ESOTERIC PROJECT MANAGEMENT

The Development and Application of Inner Power in Management

Stutisheel

Stutisheel Oleg Lebedev

Esoteric Project Management
The Development and Application of Inner Power in Management

Second Edition, March 2016

This book reveals the author's experiences with the synthesis of meditation practice and project management techniques. It covers topics that usually go unnoticed in classical training and materials on project management, including developing a vision, transcending time, leadership from a spiritual point of view and the development of inner strength, intuition and receptivity as necessary elements in successful management.

Cover design and layout: Andrey Potapov
Editors: Hladini Wilson, Sarita Earp
Bird drawings by Sri Chinmoy

For additional information please visit
www.Stutisheel.org

ISBN-13: 978-1508954118
ISBN-10: 1508954119

ABOUT THE AUTHOR

Stutisheel Oleg Lebedev is the first man from post-Soviet countries to finish the longest certified footrace in the world—The Self-Transcendence 3,100-Mile Race held each year in New York City. He has completed the race nine times, with a fastest time of 48 days 3 hours 57 minutes and 19 seconds (2014). He has been practicing meditation and self-discovery under the guidance of Sri Chinmoy for more than 23 years.

By profession, Stutisheel is a process improvement manager, a quality and project manager. He obtained his MA in Computer Science from the Moscow Institute for Physics and Technology. During more than 20 years of project management he has completed a number of large commercial projects. Among these were planning the construction of the Thermal Power Plant in Hrazdan, Armenia; implementation of project management software for the Lukoil oil refinery in Perm, Russia; the launch of an Internet portal for the Ukrainian national lottery; and certification for the fifth maturity level (CMMI ML5) of the IT company EPAM Systems in Szeged, Hungary.

Stutisheel has also carried out a number of successful social projects, including coordinating the first running of the Sri Chinmoy Oneness-Home Peace Run—a global torch relay—in Western Ukraine; organization of the international Songs of the Soul concert at the October Palace in Kyiv; coordinating the annual Ukrainian national 24-hour championship race in Kyiv; and organizing meditation training courses. He is a motivational speaker and a frequent lecturer on meditation in the Ukraine and internationally.

CONTENTS

EXERCISE LIST

INTRODUCTION

THIS BOOK IS BASED on many years' experience in esoteric project management, including daily application of these approaches. The idea behind the book is to expand the classical approach to management by developing a range of inner qualities through meditation and spiritual practice. If you look at the science of project management as the construction of a beautiful frame or shape, the inner component provides the interior.

Having worked in project management for more than 20 years, and having completed a lot of training courses, I have often found myself thinking that all the beautiful formulas, graphs and approaches are often incomplete in real life. This is not because they are wrong, but because quite often they do not reflect an integral approach that includes the inner dimension.

After practicing meditation for three decades, I began to look for answers to these problems inside myself. Once, while sitting in a course on Change Management provided by Carnegie Mellon University, I began to think that the classical approach to project management could benefit from the addition of inner qualities to help ensure that all these beautiful theories will work. Everyone can agree that willpower, the ability to remain calm under stress, insight and intuition can make an enormous contribution to effective management. But few, if any, books on project management address the development of these capaci-

ties. At the same time, books on meditation don't discuss project management.

In this book, I have tried to address the main areas of project management and discuss the improvements that could result from applying the appropriate inner qualities. The result is an interesting synthesis of meditation and project management. Or, to put it another way, the application of spiritual practices to project management. This is my concept of Esoteric Project Management.

The spiritual practices and meditation exercises that I refer to in this book are taken for the most part from the works of my teacher, Sri Chinmoy. And of course, I have verified them in my own life.

Stutisheel
Kyiv, 2014

SETTING THE GOAL

Where Does a Project Really Begin?

THE CLASSICAL DEFINITION OF A PROJECT is: "a temporary endeavour undertaken to create a unique product, service or result."[1]

Many activities fall under this definition. Classical project management training approaches project implementation by breaking a project into stages, setting up dependencies, assigning responsibilities and so on.

The topics I want to discuss go deeper than technical analysis, which certainly helps clarify the question "How?" I want to address the questions of "What?" and "Why?"

In 1995 I participated in a training course in Washington, DC for Ukrainian project managers organized by the Economic Development Institute of the World Bank. I listened wide-eyed to the many theorists and practitioners who shared their experiences.

Since taking that course, I always try to look at the big picture and to ask myself, "Why am I doing this?" (I address the question of motivation later on: "Why do people do what they

do?") Many experts say that a project receives life from the Vision of the end result. But that begs the question of how to create a powerful Vision that can guide and strengthen an entire project. This is a subject on which the science of project management remains mute.

Most people are preoccupied with getting a job, and planning their career and financial growth. They plan to purchase a car, build a home and so on. But on the deepest level, we strive to get joy from life, to be happy.

In my own life, on several occasions I found that even after achieving a goal by breaking through walls and making Herculean efforts, I got little or no satisfaction from the results.

On the one hand, it turned out the deadlines for which we had made every possible effort turned out later not to be so critical. On the other—and this is worse—the goals to which I aspired in my business projects or my private life were losing their relevance, both for me and my customers.

The question of what the customer needs or what the market needs is more specific than asking "Why am I doing this?" or "What goal will give us satisfaction in life?" It cannot be found without self-examination. Opinion polls, marketing analyses, ratings and other studies simply pale in comparison to what we can do with our developed inner capacities. We can open the door to our inner world to find our purpose, our mission on Earth. Moreover, with this Vision comes the power to implement it. This is an extremely powerful experience.

Stop the Mind

What does it take to obtain such a Vision? Paradoxically, we need to stop the mind. While the mind is a pretty good instrument for ordering our outer life and implementing our dreams, it is absolutely inappropriate for receiving a Vision, the embodiment of which brings to us not fleeting pleasure, but lasting satisfaction.

Sometimes we can have a very lofty dream, which we might call "prophetic." It can give us answers to our questions and aspirations. But do we have the capacity to take these messages from above or within, that is, from a higher or deeper divine reality, as the foundation of our conscious life? We can develop this ability to receive these hints from Above. Actually, everyone can do this, because the relationship between our inner world and today's material needs is absolutely natural. The capacity to tune in to the inner wisdom is given to us by the Creator Himself. You do not need to be a psychic or a clairvoyant—you just have to have a receptive heart. It is only necessary to wake up and feel this burning necessity to find your true Goal and Mission in life. Once you have it, you can move forward with your attempts to connect inwardly. The best way to do that is simply to meditate.

A quiet mind is the first result of a good meditation. Calming the mind—not to speak of stopping it—is an extremely difficult task. We are constantly thinking. Even when we are asleep, thoughts continue in our mind, usually expressed in our dreams. The main thing is not to give up! A good signal that you are on the right track is if you have more peace after you do a meditation exercise. You may start to smile or think positive thoughts about somebody—quite different than before the exercise. You will have a more positive attitude.

AUM.1 Exercise to calm the mind

Now for the exercises. There are many ways to stop the mind. I will mention only a few. According to my meditation teacher, Sri Chinmoy, these are more than enough ways for everyone.[2]

1. One way is to repeat the name of God or a particular mantra, which is a sacred word or incantation. When we repeat a mantra or God's Name, there is a continuous flow. If what we are repeating is "God, God, God," then inside the repetition we will forget ourselves. Then the mind stops.

2. Another way is to see the mind as a material object. We can take a material object and put it anywhere we want, or throw it the farthest possible distance, according to our strength. So either we can grab the mind like a material object and throw it far away, or we can put the mind in a place where it will not bother us. If a mischievous child is bothering us, we can put him into a corner and warn him not to move. We can do that to the mind also.

3. A third way is to totally forget about the existence of the mind and feel that we are only the heart. It is not enough to say, "I have a heart." We have to say, "I am the heart, I am the heart!" Then the qualities of the heart will permeate the entire being

and automatically the mind will stop.

When we do these exercises regularly, we allow the deeper realities that embody our heart and soul to come to the fore and to operate in our life. They are well aware of our goals and mission. Allow them to reveal this treasure to you. Our spiritual heart has the ability to picture our life as a whole. This ability is foreign to our mind. The mind specializes in dividing reality into parts and analyzing each part. However, we can call on the mind for the implementation of our dreams.

It may take time to begin to feel the spiritual heart and then to learn how to explore the world with its help. But the effort is more than worth it. We cannot even imagine what a rich inner world we have!

Extremes On the Path To Enlightenment

I discovered yet another way to calm the mind and dive deep into myself: long-distance running. Over the past ten years I have been participating in the longest footrace in the world—the Self-Transcendence 3,100-Mile Race. Each time I run the race, the experience is so rich and I have so many discoveries I feel that I am living through several lives! During heavy exertion, the mind automatically calms down and you get access to your real life. You become vividly aware of what life-activities are truly essential. This impulse to write book is the result of just such an inner revelation...

So with faith in ourselves, let's begin the journey!

THE TEAM

People Are the Most Important Part of a Project

EXPERIENCED PROJECT MANAGERS will say that the most important part of a project is the people involved in it. The quality of work, the application of relevant knowledge and many other aspects depend on the team. So all proper management techniques have to be based on the ability to work with people. It follows that the main question is the selection of the project team and the right motivation.

How is this process organized in most companies? After determining the structure of activities and tasks, management defines the responsibilities, roles, necessary skills and qualifications. If the right skills cannot be found inside the company, it may be necessary to undertake a training program or to hire people outside the company. If new workers are sought, interviews are conducted and, with luck, candidates with the needed skills can be found.

But it often happens that some aspect of a new worker's personality was not discovered during his or her interviews, and that the person works slowly or develops conflicts with other members of the team. It can be said that only experience can determine whether a person is suitable for a job or not. I would like to share my views on how to form a project team.

We want to know as much as possible about a job candidate. Typically this is accomplished with various tests and interviews. But if, in addition to this formal approach, we can consciously use our "intuitive" side and try to sense the person, then at the very first meeting we can grasp the candidate's strengths and weaknesses. Here, I am referring to sensing with the spiritual heart (anahata chakra). By nurturing this subtle inner centre, we can develop this amazing ability. We will find that no one can offer more insight than our spiritual heart. After more than twenty years of meditation, quite often I encounter situations when I feel faster than I understand. In fact, the speed with which one can grasp knowledge through the spiritual heart, with its capacity of identification with another person, is simply amazing. It is many times faster than our mind. But since the spiritual heart is not developed in most people, at first it should be used together with standard interviews and other formal techniques.

AUM.2 Concentration exercise

Concentration can help develop the ability to perceive the

surrounding world through the heart. The following exercise is suitable for most people. By concentrating on a dot or following the movement of our breath, we can completely identify with it. Then when we concentrate on other people or events, we are able to capture their very essence. For a real Master, it takes one moment to concentrate and learn all about a person. But this level of mastery takes years of practice (and even many lifetimes). This is the first step:

"Make a small black dot on the wall and stand six or seven feet away, focusing your attention on it. Try not to see the white wall around you. See only the black dot. After five or ten minutes try to enter into that dot and feel that you have become the dot itself. You are not something else or someone else. You are inside that dot. Finally, pierce the wall with your focus of concentration. Go right through the wall and beyond it. From that point, look back and try to see your original self, the person who was standing in front of the wall looking at the dot. Once you are successful with this exercise, the mind can never act like a naughty child. At that time, the mind becomes a most faithful servant of the soul and concentration becomes quite easy."[3]

Motivation

Once, when I first started to coordinate the international Oneness-Home Peace Run in the Ukraine in 1997, a problem arose in the Western Ukraine. Five days before the scheduled start in downtown Kiev we still had not found a bus for the team. The situation was critical because the run could not take place without a bus. But there were three people whose hearts were burning to make the project a success. These three developed an inner feeling the Peace Run had already taken place; that it was completed. It was as if we had a glimpse of the future. We gained tremendous confidence from this and felt that we would succeed. And we did! This experience gave me a very important lesson about how three hearts burning with enthusiasm could pave the way for the success of a torch relay of almost 1,000 km (600 miles).

For a team to work closely together, and to understand one another wordlessly, burning hearts are necessary.

In Maslow's well-known hierarchy of needs, he states that every person seeks to satisfy his or her own needs—both material (food, home, money) and non-material (communication, love, self-expression, recognition and so on.) It is worth noting that material needs rank relatively low in this hierarchy. Maslow said that the strongest motivation to work comes from self-fulfilment and the expression of creativity. From a deeper point of view, this is exactly what I mean by "burning."

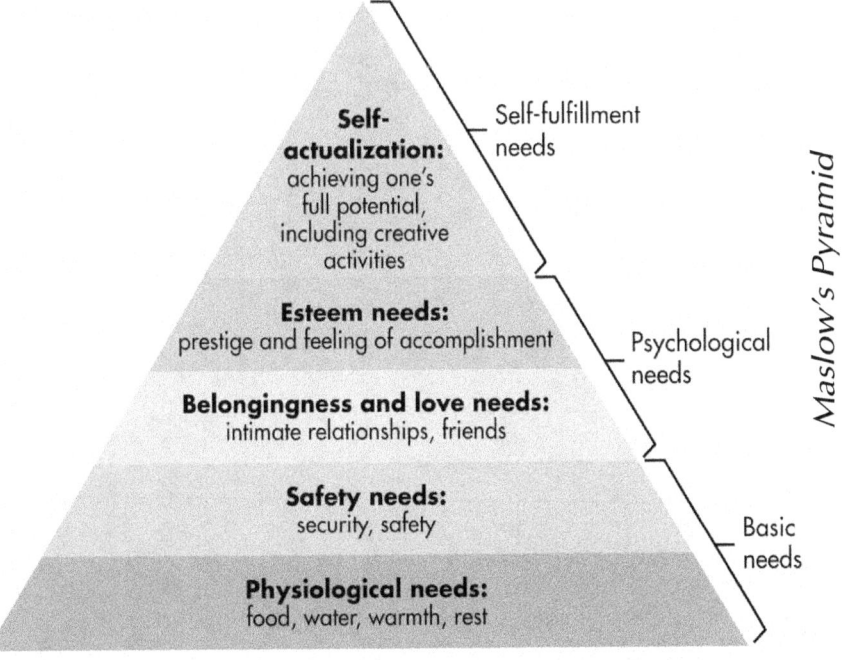

In general, we can say that when a person sees that his own needs and desires are consistent with the goals and objectives of a project, he accomplishes the desired activity with great interest and dedication.

THE SECRET OF SUCCESS

"To Serve and to Never Get Tired—Is Love"[4]

IF MATERIAL GAIN AND PROSPERITY are a project's main goals, then problems, delays and conflicts will always occur. The reason is that this is not a natural goal for humans. If you insist on making material wealth your number one goal, then you should be ready to achieve this goal separately from your own happiness. But if your goal is the implementation of a vision from deep within, the right people will appear at the right time and financing will be provided. Finally, as a by-product of this project, you will be able to make a profit and everything else you need to lead a normal life. It is a law that if there is a balance between our inner peace and outer activity, our lives will improve and we will experience lasting happiness. One of the most powerful and inspiring motives for outer activity is service to others. In fact, teamwork is essential to human happiness. Here is a series of aphorisms from famous people who dedicated their lives to others.

There is joy in transcending self in order to serve others.
Mother Teresa

Only a life lived for others is a life worthwhile.

Albert Einstein

We make a living by what we get. We make a life by what we give.

Winston S. Churchill

When one human being reaches out to help another human being ...he touches God.

Walt Whitman

No one is useless in this world who lightens the burdens of another.

Charles Dickens

For it is in giving that we receive.

Francis of Assisi

Everybody can be great, because everybody can serve. You don't have to have a college degree to serve. You don't have to make your subject and your verb agree to serve. You don't have to know about Plato and Aristotle to serve. You don't have to know Einstein's theory of relativity to serve. You don't have to know the second theory of thermodynamics in physics to serve. You only need a heart full of grace, a soul generated by love.

Martin Luther King

On a typical training course, the necessity of serving others or oneness with the world are rarely mentioned as key strategies for success. I also would like to quote one aphorism, which to me is the open secret of life's success. Everlasting. Think about it:

Whatever you are doing,
If you can feel oneness
With other human beings,
With the world,
Then you will be successful
Far beyond your own imagination.
Sri Chinmoy[5]

LEADERSHIP

What's Missing in Classical Leadership?

WE ARE ALL USED TO THINKING that a leader is the person in front and that everyone else is following. Anyone who has led a project with more than one or two participants has been faced with the challenge of how to direct, plan, monitor and coordinate. But to me, this is only the surface reality. Let's look at the issue from a slightly different angle. In my experience as a manager, I have encountered situations where I did everything in accordance with classical project management techniques: I allocated sub-projects, assigned responsibility according to experience and interests, set goals and tried to develop a consensus among the team on the importance of the project. But—people would not listen. Attention waned during meetings and we failed to make any of the decisions necessary for the progress of the project. However, there were other projects—fortunately, greater in number—when I did not give all the details in words, but I felt a tremendous confidence and inner strength that kept the project on track. I was very pleased to read in Power and Influence, a book by John Kotter of Harvard Business School, the following statement:

Few managers realise that the power in an organisation comes from inner leadership, rather than position or force.[6]

I also came to the conclusion that when you have inner strength, the external techniques that are commonly prescribed allow you to effectively guide it and apply it where it is needed. For example, you would find ways to inspire others to ignite their own burning desire to work and continue as long as necessary, and so on. The charismatic authority of a manager often creates tension and disharmony in a team. A more in-depth approach, one based on inner strength rather than star power, can lead people to work intensely but harmoniously. The very source of inner strength is peace and harmony.

Leadership Techniques

Classical project management offers suggestions on how to work with people, solve conflicts, hold discussions and so on.

Here is a selection of these techniques:

- **Do not vote on issues**. Voting divides a group into winners and losers and can lead to disputes rather than rational discussion.

- **Do not foster competition between team members**. In any project the entire team has to win or no one does.

- **Listen carefully to what others say**. This is the outstanding practice of successful teams.

- **Make sure that everyone, especially the shy members, express themselves**.

- **Be positive and friendly**.

- **Define the objectives of any meeting**.

- **Focus on the established objectives** during all aspects of the project.

These suggestions raise one essential question: how often does knowledge of all these techniques help achieve a project's goals? For example, how often does knowing the importance of a positive approach prevent us from coming down on someone who has made a mistake—and thus ultimately destroying his value to the team? How often, despite having been taught that teamwork is most effective when all the members participate, have we taken the time to listen to the least assertive? How often can we admit our own mistakes before they damage a project?

These considerations lead us to look at our inner accomplishments and the development of the inner qualities a leader needs to make the execution of a project successful and harmonious.

Esoteric Leadership

Esoteric leadership is critical if we are to *develop* in ourselves the qualities that are described in classical project management and that are necessary to work with a team successfully. Take, for example, the development of inner strength. I call this the "core" of a person. I have had many experiences that have convinced me that inner strength is based on inner peace and confidence. I would like to explain this in more detail. The confidence that I'm talking about is different from ambition and self-confidence. What I am describing is a feeling that comes from deep within and that nourishes outer actions with power. It is an internal state that a person is able to create.

You can draw an analogy to the different types of smiles. Often you will find a salesman who smiles at you mechanically. Although he is mouthing the right words, you can feel his insincerity. This is one example of form without content. Alternatively, there are sincere smiles that simply attract and inspire, although the person may be saying next to nothing. This is an example of the ideal internal state—a spiritual force.

Have you ever wondered why so many superheroes in the movies behave calmly and confidently in the most critical situations? It is because—even at a subconscious level—we have an established image of a wise and experienced person as calm, shooting directly at the "target." Inner peace makes order out of the chaos in our minds and thus in our actions as well. It is no secret that 99% of the decisions (if not all) that we make while we are in an unbalanced state are wrong. This is because when we are restless or unbalanced, we are functioning at the surface of our being. In this state of consciousness we cannot grasp a situation in its entirety. As we all know, the true answers are "at the bottom."

Folk wisdom says, "A leader always stays behind. Any shepherd will tell you this." This should be the position of the leader of any successful team, because it helps nurture the capacities of all the project members. We must learn to encourage all the talents and abilities of the project participants to come to the fore. Then, work on the project can be intense and harmonious at the same time. But to do this, we need to put the greatest emphasis on the positive aspects of our own nature and on that of others. It is difficult to overestimate the importance of encouragement and inspiration. The ability to see the positive aspects of others' personalities is evidence of great wisdom, experience and skill.

Perhaps the most important consideration in managing a

project is to realize that, since people are the key players in a project, the successful operation of a project depends on relations among people. Any approach based on modern science will only be able to take a snapshot of the actual picture. To understand and manage the entire situation, it is necessary to go beyond the ability of the mind to separate and analyse. In other words, a manager needs to calm the mind to take advantage of the ability of the spiritual heart to identify and feel oneness.

From the spiritual point of view, the secret of effective leadership is the realisation of inseparable oneness with others. The one who can lead with the power of the heart is the real leader. Furthermore, a person who can use the analytical mind as a tool of the heart will be a perfect leader, one who can manifest ancient wisdom with ultramodern methods. These qualities can and should be developed.

AUM.3 Exercise for the development of peace

On the surface of the sea are multitudes of waves, but the sea is not affected below. In the deepest depths, at the bottom of the sea, it is all tranquility. So when you start meditating, try to feel your own inner existence first. That is to say, the bottom of the sea: calm and quiet. Feel that your whole being is surcharged with peace and tranquility. Then let the waves come from the outside world. Fear, doubt, worry—the earthly turmoils—will all be washed away, because inside is solid peace. You cannot be afraid of anything when you are in your highest meditation. Your mind is all peace, all silence, all oneness. If thoughts or ideas want to come in, you control them with your inner peace, for they will not be able to affect you. Like fish in the sea, they jump and swim but leave no mark on the water. Like birds flying in the sky, they leave no trace behind them. So when you meditate, feel that you are the sea, and all the animals in the sea do not affect you. Feel that you are the sky, and all the birds flying past do not affect you. Feel that your mind is the sky and your heart is the infinite ocean. That is meditation.[7]

In addition to the above-mentioned exercise, if you can look at the setting sun for five to twenty minutes (being careful not to allow any thoughts in the mind) then your whole being will be flooded with golden peace, naturally and spontaneously.

Thinking Out Loud

Mother Teresa had the following on her business card:

The fruit of Silence is Prayer

The fruit of Prayer is Faith

The fruit of Faith is Love

The fruit of Love is Service

The fruit of Service is Peace.

MANAGING CREATIVITY

The Problem of the Creative Personality

HAVE YOU EVER WONDERED why some people succeed and others experience failure, despite the fact that they all studied the same books with the same teachers? It seems to me that the answer lies in the ability to solve problems using a non-standard approach. Those who can find an unusual solution to a problem—whether in business, creativity, sports or other areas—often continue and proceed immeasurably further.

At this point, I cannot help but pay tribute to the Moscow Institute of Physics and Technology, where I studied, because non-standard approaches are strongly encouraged and welcomed there.

But oddly enough, creative, imaginative people are less likely to fit in at many companies or with society. For example, talented software developers are less likely to document their code adequately. We can say that, on the one hand, this type of bright individual is a pillar of progress in life. On the other hand, they often "fall out of the nest" and can get involved in difficult circumstances and situations. Being original or different from others is often synonymous with "being dangerous." While a postgraduate, I became interested in this problem and even wrote my thesis on Managing Creativity. Many of the findings in that paper have been confirmed during my career as a manager.

Can Creativity Be Managed?

Following rules and established procedures is the opposite of fostering creativity. The motivation to create lies in the innate wish of people to know themselves, to realise their potential. This is apparent throughout human life with its desire to grow, develop and gain experience and to express and manifest every ability. This impulse can be deeply buried under psychological inhibitions, but it exists in all people, and is just waiting for conditions for its release and manifestation.

The secret of managing creativity lies in creating favourable conditions for its expression. In his book Toward a Theory of Creativity, Carl Rogers8 describes an environment conducive to creativity. He emphasises that creativity cannot be forced. It should be given an opportunity for it to grow. This can be done most successfully by providing for two factors: psychological safety (X) and psychological freedom (Y).

These conditions are:

X1. The acceptance of the individual as unconditionally worthwhile. This acceptance comes from unconditional faith in a person, regardless of his position. When a person feels this, he can function in an atmosphere of safety. This enables him to experiment to find himself in new and spontaneous ways. He begins to create.

X2. Establishing an atmosphere where there is no external evaluation. When an individual finds himself in an environment

where he is not subject to evaluation by any external standards, he gains a sense of unlimited freedom. Evaluation and assessment are always threats that create the need for protection. In the absence of external evaluation, an internal assessment comes to the fore in which a person asks, "Am I satisfied with my creation?" This does not mean that a person is closed to external evaluation. It just means that the main evaluation criteria lie within him, not without.

X3. Emphatic understanding. Judge people not by who they are now, but who they want to become. Accept them.

Y. Psychological freedom develops when a manager allows the complete freedom of symbolic expression. The expression of anger, for example, is usually condemned by society. However, it does permit anger to be expressed in symbolic form. Permission to be free also involves responsibility for the consequences of both one's own mistakes and achievements.

Looking at it from the esoteric side, it should be noted that the conditions of X and Y are strongly associated with a positive perception of a person and his activities, where there is no criticism. In brainstorming meetings, for example, there is a phase when everything is written down, even the most unrealistic and "crazy" ideas—with absolutely no criticism.

I often find that a critically minded person who has succeeded in achieving his own goals and who pours a sea of criticism and doubt on others is not happy himself. In this situation, we can say that everyone is a loser. On the other hand, a person who tries to see the positive qualities in others and works to bring them to the fore receives satisfaction long before reaching his goal. A positive approach is absolutely essential in the management of creativity.

AUM.4 Exercises for developing a positive approach

1. The first exercise is to enter a calm and peaceful state and then try to dive into our spiritual heart (See AUM.1 Exercise). Write down three very positive and strong qualities of your worst enemy—or the person who causes you the most problems.

In my training courses on holistic development of the personality, after this exercise many of my students began to view their so-called enemies quite differently. One student said to me: "I have found that I do not know the person with whom I have conflict most of the time at work..." We should get to know others better.

2. In the second exercise, try to imagine what flower is most similar to the person with whom you have "problems." You will be amazed at your discovery! For a while, try to retain the sense that your enemy is not a person in front of you, but a flower. In the future when you are dealing with this person, imagine that you are talking to a flower. Even if you say nothing, the person will feel a positive attitude and encouragement.

Instead of a Summary

Clearly, in today's society there are difficulties in making creativity free and spontaneous. Nevertheless, it can be done. It should be remembered that people create to satisfy their hunger for satisfaction and self-discovery. That is why any set of standard techniques will fail when it comes to inspiration and creativity. Creative people march to their own drum and seek their own, deeply hidden rewards. They usually do not respond to the types of rewards that managers often use to motivate people to work.

Recently in one of my own management courses, I used poetry in an exercise to develop creative abilities. We did a visualisation exercise in which we tried to remember one happy episode from our childhood, when we just jumped with joy. I asked the participants to relive this incident and to try to feel like happy children and then try to write down their feelings. As a result, some students wrote their first poem!

Everyone has abilities. But quite often we simply do not develop them or practice them. So this type of exercise can be an excellent tool to reach a higher plane of consciousness, where it is easier to find solutions to problems. It can be a simple and beautiful way to solve difficult problems. During this exercise for my students, I often find that I get the inspiration to express my feelings, too.

Here are some of the results of these exercises.

Spring drops—in my heart.

But outside—beginning of the winter.

My soul with the spring flowering—

greeting the sunbeam.

A mortal body in early December languishing,
struggling to stay awake.

Alexander

Strength—in your hands, in the wings—the wind.

The sun rises, its rays warm.

I do not remember now where is south,

where is north.

Feel the flight—you too will become warmer.

Maxim

I am like a little golden child.

I pray to You:

I want to be with You in all times.

You do not hurry to reveal Yourself,

But sending Your Love to me.

At once I want to be Your Reality-Dream.

You are changing my life carefully.

And I am dreaming with the burning heart:

You—I, I—You.

You, only You.

Stutisheel

NONSTANDARD SOLUTIONS

All Genius Is Simple!

TO CONTINUE THE THEME ON MANAGEMENT of creativity, I was reminded recently of a story about the time when Sri Chinmoy was heavily involved in weightlifting. At his request, one of his students, named Unmilan, designed unique machines to strengthen specific muscles.

One of the machines was used for hand presses, in which Sri Chinmoy lifted weights overhead from a standing position. When the machine was finished, Sri Chinmoy tried it out and found the range of motion for the hand was too short, so it was necessary to lower the weight. Unmilan, without thinking twice, got ready to shorten the four metal poles of the machine. Then Sri Chinmoy exclaimed that all he had to do was to put a mat under his feet!

We have heard it said that all genius is simple! Here is a way to develop this most ingenious simplicity. Many people believe that progress moves from the simple to the complex. In biology this is called the evolution of the species.

However, this idea is not necessarily correct. During the Earth's evolution, many plants and animals have evolved simpler forms, and have been able to thrive. In connection with our own lives, as we become more "mature," the challenges we face and our reactions to them seem to become more complicated. However, this might be an illusion. We see ourselves as the ultimate result of the creation of nature. And the ultimate creation within ourselves is the mind. But from the spiritual point of view, the mind must be transcended before it can be used effectively to attain progressive goals. In other words, there are many levels of development above the mind. On these levels, giving joy to others and receiving joy from life become simple and natural.

Sri Chinmoy said repeatedly that it is necessary to go beyond the mind to dive into the spiritual heart. He also offered a variety of exercises to help do this. I remember well him saying that if we could feel that we are happy children, we would not need to meditate or do spiritual exercises at all. The heart of a child—this is the answer.

If you would like to look at a problem or the world from a different, unique angle, and see hidden opportunities—see it through the eyes of a child, a child's heart. If a child asks us a question, sometimes we are stuck for an answer and we embark on very long and complicated explanations.

Why didn't all monkeys evolve into humans?

How were people able to agree what words to use to name what things?

Why do people have five fingers?

Can microbes see each other?

Is it possible to outrun the sun?

Why are there 365 days in the year?

Children behave spontaneously and are not limited to the preconceived ideas, models and explanations of adults. So if we want a non-standard solution, a child's view of reality might help. As I said earlier, all genius is simple! Adults just need to make an effort to calm their minds that are constantly thinking standard ideas. This is an integral approach—it can even be a way of life. The order of the day should be music, dynamism and spontaneous joy.

It is difficult to become a child at one's sweet will, especially if you are a modern adult. Here is a helpful exercise.

AUM.5 Becoming a child

"Try to feel that you are a child, no matter how old you are in earthly age. A child's mind is not developed. When he is twelve or thirteen his mind starts functioning on an intellectual level, but before that he is all heart. Whatever he sees, he feels is his own. He identifies spontaneously. This is what the heart does. When you feel that you are a child, immediately feel that you are standing in a flower garden. This flower garden is your heart. A child can play in a garden for hours. He will go from this flower to that flower, but he will not leave the garden, because he will get joy from the beauty and fragrance of each flower. Inside you is the garden, and you can stay within it for as long as you want. In this way you can meditate on the heart by becoming a child."[3]

MIND MANAGEMENT

From Order Within to Power Without

IN THIS CHAPTER we will talk about thought control, or mind management.

I have repeatedly pointed out that in project management, in addition to effective skills and knowledge, it is extremely important for a manager to have inner power—to be positive, creative and dynamic, and to be able to synthesise all parts of a project. In fact, we cannot manage projects well unless we can manage ourselves. A manager needs access to inner reserves, which are far superior to anything a person could have in the outer world. When we try to manage ourselves, the first thing we often face is that our thoughts are in turmoil. From the spiritual point of view, confusion and chaos in the mind result in anxiety and inner weakness. (I cannot resist pointing out that in physics, the stable state of a system is called the "resting equilibrium".) In our everyday life, we rarely notice or think about how much the world of our thoughts affects our outer actions, our performance and our efficiency. While we might say that we have a headache or cannot concentrate, in reality our state reflects our inability to resist the external stresses that have such a detrimental effect on us.

For many years, I have been participating in the longest footrace in the world—the Self-Transcendence 3,100-Mile Race. When I ran this race for the ninth time, in the summer of 2012, I realized as never before how much the body depends on the attitude of the mind. In fact, most of the diseases and ailments that attack us try to enter into us through our mind first. We might notice that something is wrong. But if we do not start to react to this awareness and work on it, there is every chance that soon the body will get sick. The runners in the 3,100-Mile Race use a powerful visualisation technique that helps prevent emerging injuries to penetrate the body and develop further.

That summer I recognized an amazing connection between the mind and the body. Starting with my first 3,100-Mile Race in 2004 I had two major problems: the heat (it got up to 104∘F in the shade) and the full moon. Of course, there were plenty of other difficulties, but these two were the most serious. Over the years, I began to develop an attitude in which my mind was extremely determined to conquer the heat and keep running. As a result of this inner commitment, I began to feel that it was almost as if I was covered by a protective film. I stopped feeling the heat so much and I was able to continue. Comparing my recent races with the earliest ones, I clearly see that I have made considerable progress with being able to run in the extreme heat. While there are certainly many outer techniques for running in the heat, involving nutrition and special sunblock equipment, it was my inner determination that made it possible for me to reach a new level of performance during the very hot periods.

It turned out to be much more difficult to resolve my issue with the full moon. Mysteriously, I have found that my internal organs react when the moon is full by refusing to work properly. It affects my liver especially. Every full moon I tried to

break through this problem with inner determination, and several times it almost worked. But often I was caught by the "tail" of the moon's influence and got very weak again. One summer, two full moons took place during the 52 days of the race (2012). As the full moon approached, I slowly began to panic because of the physical collapse that it presaged. In this fearful mental state, it was as if my body had received a command to become weak and was obediently fulfilling it. Ironically, the race doctors were always able to identify perfectly logical reasons for my problems. But the underlying reason was not on the physical plane! On the eve of the second full moon, I made every effort to resist any reaction. I tried to ignore the calendar, to be positive and to intensify my visualizations of strength and speed. But then, on the day of the full moon, there was a general announcement that someone brought sweets to the track in honour of the full moon! My mind got a lethal dose that I couldn't resist. For several days I could not run. I became one of the walking dead.

I was amazed at the way a thought could paralyse the body during a race! And if we look at our daily lives–particularly at work—we often find ourselves paralysed with fear, doubt, suspicion and other mental poisons. Thus it is extremely important to learn how to control the mind and not to give it any opportunities to develop negativity and limit our capacities.

At one point during the race, I experienced a unique feeling—everything was breathing! The sky, the trees, the houses, everything living and nonliving; everything and everyone had their own rhythm of breathing, but all were connected with the one Source from which all were breathing... Recently, I was surprised to find this experience described in a passage on pranayama, which is an extremely important practice involving control of the breath and, as a result, for the mind.

AUM.6 Practice for proper breathing

All of you are breathing in and out. Please try to observe whether you are breathing primarily through your left nostril or through your right nostril. Those of you who are breathing in through the left nostril, please repeat the word moon, and those who are breathing through the right, please repeat the word sun.

If you want to change your fate, there is a most significant and most effective method of doing this. During the day or night, when you observe that your left nostril is functioning and not your right, then try to concentrate or meditate on the moon for a few minutes. You will get the moon's qualities: peace, serenity and subtle bliss. When you observe that the right nostril is functioning, then concentrate on the sun. You are bound to get the qualities of the sun: dynamism and divine power. But if you misuse this power, if you do not aspire for dynamic and energising power, then it becomes aggression; and if you misuse this peace or subtle bliss, then immediately inertia, lethargy and idleness will attack you and try to take full control of your life. When you feel inert, when you do not feel like doing anything, if you observe, you will see that it is the left nostril that is

functioning. But when you are energetic, when you want to do something, at that time it is the right one.

When you do heavy exercise, you will see that both nostrils are functioning equally. When both the nostrils are functioning, at that time divine Peace and divine Power are functioning simultaneously in you. But you have to be conscious of them and invoke them more and more. Every day you are breathing. Try to observe your breath in your day-to-day activities. Even if you can spend five minutes out of each hour being conscious of your breathing, that will be wonderful. Daily if you use the breath properly, you can bring in more power and peace to illumine your Ignorance.[9]

TIME MANAGEMENT

The Problem of Deadlines

IT IS COMPARATIVELY RARE TO FIND projects that have completed on schedule. Of course, there are many reasons for this. Classic project management explores this problem and suggests using technical and organizational techniques to meet the deadline. The Critical Path Method concentrates resources and efforts on the longest path of the project.

I would like to look at the issue more deeply, including esoteric management approaches.

Often something goes wrong with our willingness to work:

• We got up on the wrong side of the bed (Friday can't come soon enough!)

• Family problems (How can I work with so much stress?)

• A sick child (I cannot work when I am constantly worrying.)

• Being slow by nature—"bulldozer type"—as I call people who start slowly, but then continue to do everything precisely and accurately.

How can you take all this into account when planning a project and its budget? It has been proposed that 10% should be added to the duration of any project to allow for unforeseen circumstances. This is a good practice, but it does not solve the problem of how to meet deadlines. Perhaps you have been in a situation where you were applying the greatest possible effort and pressuring others to try to meet a target date only to have the priorities and objectives completely changed or to have a critical delivery postponed beyond your control. When that happened, you probably indulged in all your negative emotions without restraint.

It happens often. In my opinion, we cannot proceed effectively without discovering the underlying cause for these events and activities in the inner world. We need to go beyond the surface.

Beyond the Boundary of Time

In one Indian tract I read a description of time that completely revolutionised my way of thinking. A yogi had an experience in which he saw the boundaries of time and simply went beyond them. This yogi said that just as cities and countries have boundaries, time also has a limit, and you can go beyond it. Having gone beyond the boundary of time, you can perform actions that are outside of the limitations of time. To me, this was pure mysticism. But something inside me responded and felt that this was true: it is possible to do many things in the inner world without being bound by time. On the outer plane, it might appear that only a few fleeting seconds had passed, while inwardly many things were being accomplished. Later I learned that this is how spiritual Masters of the highest order can act.

In 2004, the first time I ran the 3,100-Mile Race, I had several experiences with time. Due to the long-term physical effort required during the race, the mind automatically calms down. You get access to life as it really is. A few times I found myself thinking that the time in which I live during the race is different from ordinary time, the time that I divide into hours, minutes and seconds. During the race, time is not divisible; instead, it is a continuous flow. And if you can be in harmony with this, you "flow" to your goal confidently and quickly. After I finished that race, I had the feeling that I had lived several lifetimes during that 50+ days.

Control of Yourself Equals Management of Others

Coming back to project management, often, as a result of long experience, professionals in this field can develop a level of intuition that lets them "know" in advance how or when something will happen. This quality can and should be developed consciously. With the help of certain meditation exercises, fifteen to twenty years of hands-on experience can be developed in as little as four or five years.

Let us not forget that people are the key to any project. Since most of us are quite often undisciplined, therefore what should be done in two days can take a week or more because of poor concentration, a lack of inspiration or just plain laziness. In contrast to this, I remember working with people who were simply boiling with dynamism and who could get an enormous amount of work done in an incredibly short period of time. Their dynamism was very inspiring and it led me to the following conclusion:

In order to manage others effectively, it is necessary to embody the very qualities that you expect from them: inspiration, enthusiasm, dynamism, concentration, confidence, and so on.

What will happen next is dictated by reality. But if a manager is receptive enough and can maintain an open mind and decipher the language of outer circumstances, then he can redirect the focus from one job to another in a timely fashion. He should slow down or add intensity to the performance of specific tasks as needed. This is where a manager must have the ability to immerse himself in the dynamic flow of time. Unfortunately, the mind is unable to do this. Unless a manager can use deep, internal practices in the planning and monitoring of projects, then planning efforts will often result in deadlines that are based only on external data, and therefore, quite unrealistic.

Earthly Time and Timeless Time

I look upward. I earn time. I look forward. I utilise time. I look inward. I save time. I look backward. I waste time.

~ Sri Chinmoy[10]

In our daily life, we use earthly time. It measures our actions and also can be measured itself—one hour, two hours, three hours and so on. An hour is divided into 60 minutes, and one minute contains 60 seconds. So we can divide earthly time into parts. We can arrange a time and be on time. In the morning, we wake up at 7:00 a.m. At 9:00 a.m. we can be in the office. At 11:00 p.m. we go to bed. Time regulates our actions in life. But there is also something called "timeless time." As I mentioned, I have read descriptions of timeless time written by

Indian yogis, and I was lucky to experience this time while running 3,100 miles. My experiences have made me see it as a river. This time is not divided into parts. This river flows into infinity.

The great Indian poet Rabindranath Tagore sang:

O Infinite, in the heart of the finite

You are playing Your own melodies.

In me is Your Revelation and Manifestation.

Therefore ecstasy within, ecstasy without.

The soul uses limitless time. Infinity blooms in this time. And when we become united with our soul, we can use this "timeless time"—eternal time. At the moment, this may appear to be a mystery. However, the directions to enter this "timeless time" are available to us. If we want to really learn how to manage time, we must learn to go beyond time.

No to Being Late

All of us have been late at least once in our lives. The consequences can be dire. But the more we try to control the mind and live in the heart, the fewer problems with time remain in our lives. I started practicing meditation more than twenty years ago. After some time, I began to notice changes in myself:

First, I could maintain a good mood for 365 days a year. Second, events in my life gradually began to happen flawlessly. The number of failures and mistakes I experienced began to diminish. Determination saved me at critical times and helped me to feel: "I will be on time. I can do this." (I wrote one fascinating story about how I was able to delay a Delta Airlines flight to be

on time for the start of the 3,100-Mile Race in my another book, Eat to Run.)

Now I understand that "impossible" is a word our reasoning and doubting mind is very fond of. But that word is not to be found in the dictionary of our heart and soul.

AUM.7 Exercise to stop time

Perhaps everyone has had moments in life when they felt so good that they wanted to stop time. In fact, this can be done. In my management courses, we do the following group exercise, although in a longer format. (Doing it in a group intensifies the results.) However, you can apply it to any moment in your life that you wish to capture. This will perhaps be your first conscious effort to go beyond time.

Sri Chinmoy told me about this exercise in answer to a question I asked.

1. Move your concentration from the mind to the spiritual heart, visualising, for instance, your favourite flower at the center of the chest.

2. Focus on your heartbeat, so that you can clearly hear each beat of your heart in your ears.

3. Offer your gratitude to your Creator, the Supreme, for this intense joy.

"Then time will stop and joy will continue."

I would like to add a few more thoughts on time management. We face this situation every day: I have no time. I'm late, I can't do it now. And so on. Every day we fight with time. The larger our project is, the more critical time management becomes. Often, we have no time to do everything and so we have to choose, prioritise, distribute and delegate tasks. We turn to all the techniques that we have learned in classic time management. Unfortunately, in most cases, things don't turn out the way we want.

What about trying to take this point of view?

Time can cause anxiety, fear and frustration in us, because we are working through our ego. There is always a tug of war between the ego's absurd intensity and the unknown and merciless flow of time. But if we work with our soul and for the soul, then time not only helps us, but at every moment it appears before us as a golden opportunity because our soul infallibly knows how to throw itself into the cosmic rhythm of infinite time.

~ Sri Chinmoy

We experience the tension that is born in the mind, because our mind has no capacity to realise the mystery of time. There are always limits to earthly time, and we are constantly fighting with them. But our hearts and souls have the ability to harmoniously and naturally immerse us in a heaven-free "timeless time," where all our actions take place in accordance with the universal Rhythm. This Rhythm is well acquainted with our soul. If we want to tune ourselves to be in harmony with this "timeless time," we have to go beyond the mind, which operates on earth-bound time.

The *Upanishads* say that time appeared only with the creation of the Earth. At that time, the play of a principle that is

known in science as the space-time principle began. But what was the connection between time and matter (space) before that happened? Is it possible to go beyond this chain? The first question I will leave unanswered. But as to the second, I received a powerful insight about this during the 3,100-Mile Race, when athletes run for 52 days for an average distance of 60 miles per day. I have participated ten times in this event, which is the world's longest certified foot race. I experienced an amazing transformation in my receptivity while living and competing with such extreme effort.

I already mentioned that during the race time flows differently. You cannot divide it into fragments. It is a river that flows through you. When there is such a heavy burden on the body, you feel the weight of each moment and you treasure each moment immensely. You can make friends with that flow, which carries you to your goal very harmoniously and without tension. I found that when I tried to strictly follow a daily schedule that included specific milestones, pushing myself when I was unable to meet them, the result was a lot of stress on my mind and body. And as a result I fell behind schedule. But when I was able to dive deeper into myself and remain in a good and joyful consciousness, this river of time not only carried me to my goal of a certain number of miles per day, but also freed me from tension and gave me a child's delight. In the summer of 2014 I set my personal best, running 71 miles on day 48 of the race! On that day, at 10 minutes before midnight, when I was finishing my "business day" on the road, I felt boundlessly happy and quite buoyant.

All these events gave me this idea:

One time, which we call earthly time, flows in our minds. But the real time, which is not earthbound— flows through our hearts and souls.

Heaven's last Message:
Step out of the mind's
Fleeting time
And enter into the heart's
Eternity.
~ Sri Chinmoy[5]

There are many exercises to calm the mind and allow the spiritual heart to show its strength in full power. Once again I'm referring to AUM.1 in the beginning of the book. When we develop the strength of the heart and allow it to operate in our daily lives, the issue of struggling with time goes away. Because the heart "unmistakably knows how to throw itself into the cosmic rhythm of infinite time."

For the modern busy adult—except running 3,100 miles —it may be advisable to take 10 minutes in the morning and in the evening to meditate on the heart. You will not have to wait long for the results to appear. You will see how inconsistencies fade away from your life, how you begin to succeed in serious situations and how events will mysteriously and flawlessly happen for your benefit. And all this is just an introduction to what the power of the heart can do in our life.

RISK MANAGEMENT

If You Do Not Manage Risks, They Will Manage You

TRADITIONALLY, RISK MANAGEMENT is associated with probabilities. Something might happen, but then again it might not. If nothing happens, then you are throwing money and time away. It is similar to buying car insurance: if nothing happens, you just lose money. And if that were not the case, insurance agencies would have all been out of business. However, if the event does take place and we have taken it into account, the after-effects might be less severe. In many books you will find something like the following approach to quantify the various categories of risk in a project so that they can be compared directly:

Risk	P. Probability of occurance (0-1)	I. Impact on the project (0-10)	Risk weight = P*I	Preventive actions
Delivery delays at customs	0,5	10	5	Bribe customs officials in advance :)

The risks are then prioritized according to their probability and potential impact. But, in fact, this approach leads us to follow risks: we only keep track of the consequences and try to lessen them in advance. In the esoteric approach, we learn to influence the causes of risks. We learn how to reduce the probability of the risk occurring, rather than predicting the damage from its occurrence. This is the essence.

To determine the level of impact and consider preventive action is not such a difficult task. Translating it into simpler language, a risk is a bottleneck in a project. There is a probability that something will go wrong in every project. But often we lack even the most elementary level of concentration on these "bottlenecks." If we just let things take their course, we help ensure that Murphy's Law will operate (If something can go wrong, it will go wrong). Concentration, or keeping focus on critical phases of the project, helps ensure that things will proceed smoothly.

Here is an example from the organization of the Peace Run torch relay in Ukraine. This was many years ago, when we could not afford to pay the police to accompany the relay in one region because the charges were high and our funds were limited. For several days I lived and slept with this problem. I felt enormous inner pressure to solve it.

I kept calling the local coordinators only to hear the same old news: "Nothing has changed." But then I was told that just after my previous call the police had agreed to accompany the runners throughout the entire region for free! However, if I had responded to the risk differently, by looking for funding or trying to bring political pressure on the police, I might have failed and the breakthrough would not have happened.

The second thing I would like to recommend is visualisationof the project breaking through the bottlenecks. We cannot

even imagine the extent to which enthusiastic, positive visualisationhelps to move a project forward! I would describe it as the "atomic" power. This visualisationhelps to use our true potential. At the same time it underscores the extent to which doubt—even a drop of it—can impact the success of a project. Doubt can lead to delays or even failure. Unfortunately, we often have to face doubt head-on in our lives. Both concentration and visualization, which I have briefly described, are connected with the use of inner power. This is how an esoteric approach seeks to influence outer events from within.

From Chaos to Order

The ability to pay attention to a task, issue or subject for a long time helps enormously in the ordering of our outer activities. Otherwise, we are like monkeys, jumping from one branch to another at every moment. I would like to offer my own interpretation of the law of entropy, or the Second Law of Thermodynamics. (Entropy is a measure of disorder, and maximum entropy means maximum disorder.)

In an isolated system with occurrence of spontaneous processes, entropy of the system tends to a maximum.

This holds true because the maximum entropy is a steady state for such a system. I like to draw an analogy between this law and our lives. If we do not make any effort at all, everything rushes to a state of complete disorder, or chaos, which has a stable equilibrium in nature. But human activity aims at reducing chaos, and thus it is always connected with various efforts. We can take these efforts as concentration on the problem.

I would like you to revisit an exercise to develop the ability of concentration, which I described earlier (AUM.2).

PLANNING FOR BOTTLENECKS

Key Process

IN MY PROFESSIONAL LIFE, I work on improving, optimizing and introducing processes to help move companies to new levels, primarily in the field of software development. In this field, according to the Capability Maturity Model Integration, in order to lift a company from the initial level, it is necessary to pay special attention to a number of key processes. One such process is project planning. Planning enables the company to organize activities, develop a sequence of tasks, prioritize, define responsibility and so on. This is the opposite of just following the pressures of everyday work, which is what takes place in most companies.

Very often (if not always) a company's management wants to know what its employees are doing at any given time, specifically what their workload is and how efficiently they carry it out. Management concerns itself with the big picture. Another way to describe this is as a portfolio of projects with different layouts. Oddly enough, this cannot be achieved without establishing a company-wide culture of planning. Developing a complete picture of a company's operations is always a headache for managers, especially if they are accustomed to just handing out tasks

as they arise.

Many books have been written and thousands of presentations have been made on the necessity of planning. I would like to address the topic of "bottlenecks" in planning and, as usual, to offer an expanded view of the classical project management on the subject.

Workflows

First of all, I would like to point out that rectilinear plans with clear time-divisions for phases are mostly outdated. Of course, it's easy for managers to set requirements once and never change them. Or to try to develop a piece of code that works under all conditions and through any changes. But the crazy pace of life brings with it its own corrections. Nature itself insists on a cyclical approach: night follows day, winter follows fall, and so on. So instead of a rectilinear plan, we have a spiral. And it really gets interesting when you straighten a spiral. It turns out that some activities "flow" through the entire project, or at least some of its phases. This brings us to the concept of "workflows."

Among the most important workflows are:

- Business Modelling
- Requirements Management
- Analysis and Design
- Development
- Testing
- Configuration and Change Management
- Project management

Iterations

Uncertainty at the beginning of a project results in trying to move forward in small steps, iterations, collecting more information and clarifying the customer's requirements on a piece-meal basis.

There is a more formal definition of iterations, but I want to convey just the essence. Many managers, regardless of the field in which they work, plan by iteration. They sprint forward for a week or two because they can envision what needs to be done in the immediate time frame. Then they check again and make a correction to the general plan for the following week, and so on.

Thus the wheel (or cycle) of the project rolls forward. This is called the Deming Wheel (or Cycle), which is composed of four segments:

- Planning
- Implementation/Do
- Control/Study
- Corrections/Act

One turn of the wheel constitutes one iteration of the project. This analogy summarizes the natural course of things very accurately.

In my courses I like to draw this wheel, which rolls up a hill. Obviously, because of the slope, a project can roll itself to the state of chaos without any effort. But since a project's goals rarely include chaos, it will be necessary to make an effort. This conclusion comes from the Second Law of Thermodynamics. But I will write more about this and other inputs from Nature in the following chapters.

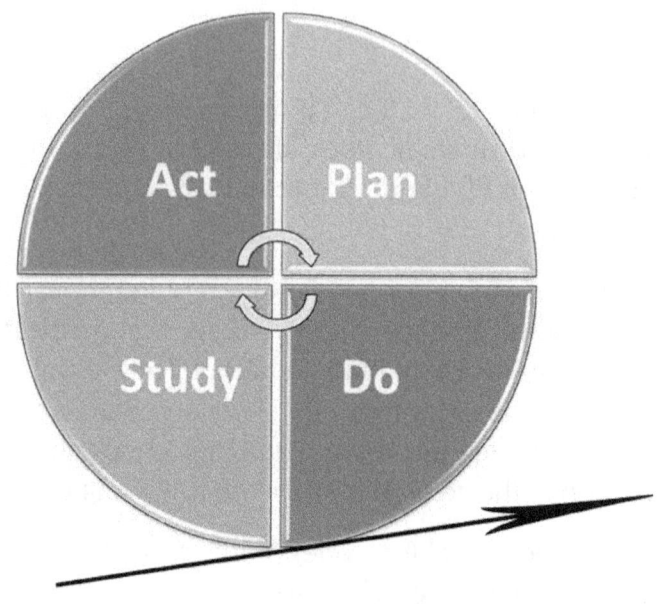

Deming's PDSA Wheel

Planning from the Final Picture

I would like to share with you some techniques that I use myself. I began by applying them to simple projects. But now, having worked in the IT industry for more than ten years, I see that the popular approach of Agile development involves attaching test scenarios to each task—to ascertain whether an application's functionality is correct or not. These scenarios reflect the final functionality as either working as expected or not working properly (happy and sad scenarios).

The essence of my approach is trying to foresee and experience the end result of your project in real time. In the process you write down what is needed to achieve the results you expect.

Consider the following example.

The task will be to organize video presentations. I'll show you the first few steps.

To carry out this task, I calm down, close my eyes and try to live the entire process in real-time...

N	Action	What needs to be done?
1	Prepare myself for the presentation	Find a quiet place where you can be alone before the presentation. Come in advance
2	I come to the room for a presentation	Reserve a room
3	There are people In the hall to whom I will make my presentation	Advertise to attract the target audience
4	Drinking water	Request a water cooler with water, cups and napkins

N	Action	What needs to be done?
5	Project the first slide	Video Projector with adapters
		A sound system, if necessary
		Screen
		Laser Pointer
		Laptop or flash drive containing the presentation
		Come in advance to set up the equipment and rehearse the presentation

These steps should continue as needed. I hope the approach is clear.

STRESS MANAGEMENT

Recipes to Overcome Stress

THE FRENETIC RHYTHM of our lifestyle often leads us to stress. Stress has become an integral part of our lives today. Of course there are many techniques for stress management. However, in this section I would like to refer not only to stress management, but also to the psychology of stress. By this I mean the inner reasons that lead to stress in our outer life.

We often say, "my job is eating me up" or "there's too much pressure in my life." Often we develop some weakness because the pressure of outer circumstances has unbalanced our lives. We need some force or power that is superior in strength to the insane pressure of life, something that will return our life to a natural and harmonious state. There is only one source that can provide us with this: inner power. I call this the inner core, where no internal or external storm can threaten our life. As Sri Chinmoy has revealed:

Peace
Is the indomitable response
To life's every challenge.
~ Sri Chinmoy[11]

Sometimes people ask me, "Isn't it boring to be calm all the time?" Usually people who ask this completely underestimate the strength and power of inner peace. By way of example, I would say that the maximum physical performance and efficiency are possible only in a state of indomitable peace. This peace is a source of one-pointed concentration and transparency of thought. This is one of the lessons I have learned from the 3,100-Mile Race.

Inner peace is the core of our life that makes us feel absolutely confident. It is interesting to note that inner peace often manifests itself in a feeling of relaxation. And oddly enough, it is in this state of relaxation, where one is free of tension, that body and spirit can unfold their greatest capacity. A tense person is bound. He is weak and vulnerable because his mental horizon and ability to act are limited. If this is the case, how can we even think about managing stress? So the first step in stress management is to relax. The question is, how?

I will share a few of the techniques that I use myself:

1. Meditation: Use meditation exercises to calm the mind. When the mind is tense, the body and emotions also become tense. Please refer to the beginning of this book where you will find a simple exercise (AUM.1).

2. Exercise. An amazing way to calm the mind is through physical exercise. The longer you can work out, the better. I notice that after only 50 minutes of continuous effort, vanity and small-mindedness disappear. Your head becomes clearer, and you understand better what to do and how to act. This is my favourite topic—I can talk about it for hours. The underlying concept is that humans were made for movement. When we deprive ourselves of movement, of pure forest air and the beauty of nature, we upset our inner balance and undermine our well-being. Then we become vulnerable to disease, stress and failure. But this can be avoided!

Another secret is that being in motion generates energy. It is only when we are active that energy comes to us. The proverb "a rolling stone gathers no moss" is a modern expression of this truism.

3. Nature. Nature contains within itself an amazing reservoir of beauty and peace. When we admire a trembling leaf, the great beauty of a sunset or the joy of the sunrise, the sound of waves or the singing of the birds, we open ourselves to the beautiful, to the natural force that makes us harmonious. We all know that. The essential issue is that we need to set priorities in our lives and discipline ourselves so that we experience Nature often enough.

4. Music. All music affects us. But there is a special type of music that can bring us balance, a surge of strength, an enduring good mood and harmony. This is the music of the heart and soul. You don't hear it often, because it requires that both the composer and the musician have the ability to enter higher planes of consciousness that will enable them to bring this heavenly music down into the hustle and bustle of our world. Sri Chinmoy's music definitely falls into this category. A good example is *Flute Music for Meditation*, which has become quite popular.

DECISION-MAKING

Penetration into the Essence of Things

DECISION-MAKING IS THE CENTRAL ISSUE, not only in project management but in every aspect of our lives. To quote an aphorism, "He who has information rules the world." I would like to modify this statement slightly.

I would add the word "authentic." Information can be of varying quality and reliability. I have always been interested in the question "What really happened?"

What really happened on 9/11 in New York? Did American astronauts actually land on the moon? Where was the Christ born and how did he actually live? Information is frequently—even deliberately—"distorted." This brings us to the question of how to get to the truth in information? This question is applicable both in our daily life and in global affairs.

But even if we are certain that our information is correct, it is not always possible to arrive at a valid solution, much less to implement one.

Thus the decision-making process can be divided into two stages: first, obtaining complete, reliable, comprehensive information and second, developing a suitable solution. Let us examine this more closely.

What Really Happened?

From time to time I give media interviews. Later on, I read the article or watch the broadcast. Quite often the media's version is not related to the interview at all! How much less reliable are events in history, that can be rewritten so easily and that lose details dramatically over time. I was happy to find many of my own thoughts in the Da Vinci Code by Dan Brown, with its perspective that history is written by the winners. Nevertheless, not everything is lost. Looking at the matter from the esoteric point of view, we can assert that all inner and outer events—even thoughts—are recorded in the "universal book," also called the Akashic Records. For truly spiritual people of a high level of consciousness, it is not difficult to "read" this book.

The bottom line is that this ability is no one's monopoly. It is not a question of limited access or different rights. People develop the ability to look into the essence of things naturally, along with their spiritual development. And complementary to the search for accurate information through external means, the ability to perceive what is going on inwardly provides amazing completeness and detail.

To give an example, at one point I was shocked to realize that the goal of the pharmaceutical industry is not people's health. Just imagine what would become of the pharmaceutical industry, pharmacy chains and medical institutions, if people no longer got sick or if they learned how to heal themselves. Assuredly, the latter is given to us by Nature itself. Unfortunately, almost all pills have side effects.

I'd also like to share my views on another common stereo-type that "truth is born from disputes." Throughout my career I have participated in many discussions and debates on various issues. I have come to the conclusion that this approach, at best, moves at a snail's pace. Even when it was possible to come to an agreement through a debate, it always left me with a bad taste in my mouth. When we argue on the mental plane of consciousness, the essential problem is that the mental plane can perceive the actual reality only very slightly. Through our mental processes we might arrive at a new model and layout of the situation, and from that make new decisions, but the underlying reality of the situation, as it existed before the dispute, continues to remain the same after the difference of opinion has been resolved. Truth is not born from disputes. Rather, it is more fully veiled by them. Truth is born in silence. It is only through the silence of the mind that we can reveal it. This applies both to the global Truth and to the truth in our everyday activities.

From my own experience I am convinced that there is a much more natural, accurate and faster way to understand the essence of things than through intellectual study. This is the approach through the identification of the spiritual heart. This ability is foreign to our mind. The mind is the master of dividing existence into parts and analyzing each one. But our spiritual heart is by nature endowed with the capacity for identification and for embracing reality as a whole. It is the heart that enables us to sympathize with others, and to feel their joys and sorrows. If we take a conscious approach to developing the qualities of the heart, then we can grasp the essence of events, the motives of human actions and the underlying causes of events, without the help of commentators, columnists or analysts. In a word, the heart enables us to see the essence of things.

I also came to the conclusion that while developing the

spiritual heart, we gradually become less influenced by the media and advertising. This happens because they influence our minds to make choices and form opinions that favour certain people and groups. I believe that highly spiritual people cannot be fooled. Genuine yogis need only a moment to see what's really going on. But if we perceive life only through the mind, we deceive ourselves. More precisely, we allow ourselves to be deceived.

With reference to those who seek to form public opinion, it is worth noting Sri Chinmoy's statement:

To falsify anything in life
Is the height
Of our stupidity.[12]

AUM.8 Exercises on Identification

"While you are placing a flower on the shrine, try to feel that this flower is reminding you of your heart, which you want to be as beautiful as the flower. You cannot see your heart, but you can look at a flower and say, 'How I wish my heart were as beautiful as this flower!'

"Then try to feel that this flower that you have placed on the shrine is breathing, the same way that your heart is taking in

your life-breath. Connect your heart-flower and the outer flower. While you are looking at the flower on the shrine, feel that your breath is entering into it. Then again, feel that the flower has entered into your heart and there it is breathing. Your heart-flower and the flower that you have placed on the shrine are going to and fro; they are constantly interchanging. The flower that is on the shrine is entering into your heart, and again it is coming out to be on the shrine.

"By seeing something with our outer eyes, we can become it. By becoming something also, we can see it. But it is far easier to see something with our outer eyes and then imagine that we are becoming that same thing on the inner plane."[13]

"If you have an intimate friend who is absolutely sympathetic to you and your inner life, you can try this with him: you have to enter into him and you have to breathe simultaneously with him. If two sincere, dedicated, aspiring souls sit together every day and practice breathing together, they will achieve the result. You should count one, two, three, and breathe in at the same time. Then stop counting. When you are breathing in, feel that he is also breathing in. Look at one another and converse through the eyes. If you can develop identification this way with two persons sitting face to face, then you can throw this same power of identification all over the entire world. Even if the person is separated from you, thousands of miles away, you can easily know what he is thinking."[14]

These exercises are keys to penetrate into the essence of things. Afterwards, you will be able to identify with a situation, another human being—anything. And you will be aware of "what really happened."

Those who are brave enough to try to know themselves can take these exercises as homework: You can experiment by focusing on and by identifying with a sunset, a tree, a candle or any other inspiring object or phenomenon. After completing the exercise, try to understand what quality is embodied in the object.

Making Forceful Decisions

It's no secret that forceful decisions are made by strong people. Or, at least, by people whose strong human qualities have come to the fore. From the esoteric point of view, it is extremely important to develop willpower, responsibility, reliability and determination along with receptivity, intuition, flexibility and an open mind. In short, we need to develop the ability to connect with our inner Vision and Power. As long as we limit ourselves to the outer aspect of decision-making, we cannot be 100% successful because we remain under the influence of fear—fear of taking responsibility, fear of failure to recognize the correct solution, and so on. In a word, we remain bound by "human factors."

From my own experience, I can say that in order to begin to develop a solution, I need to "dive" into the situation. This requires some time. It is not until you start to navigate through the specifics of the situation with your "eyes closed" that the solution begins to emerge. Once, when I was working in the project office of a bank, I heard the saying, "The devil is in the details." Without a professional background, it is quite difficult to find an effective solution.

I would like to share my personal method of dealing with a problem. I go for a run—a long one. After an hour of jogging,

the chaos in my head becomes very orderly. The mind "clears" with physical effort and as a result, quite often I am able to understand the direction I need to take to solve the problem at hand. Many strategic decisions, as well as solutions to daily problems come to me during my runs. Thus I composed my first letter to the Ukrainian Cabinet of Ministers, the approach to organize several all-Ukrainian projects became clear, and the outlines of many of my books were formed. It's a simple and effective way to get work done. I suggest you try it.

It seems to me that the feelings I have during exercise have the same source as that which I wrote about earlier: an integral Vision made possible by a calm mind and an ability to perceive a situation in its entirety that comes from the aspiring heart.

If we look at a problem from the esoteric point of view, we should remember first of all that life does not present us with any situation that is beyond our strength to resolve. And, second, if an outer problem seems to be trying to lead us into a dead end, then inwardly it is definitely aiming at the development and manifestation of our character. It is said that by solving problems in life we make progress. In fact, from the spiritual perspective, this is the sole purpose of the so-called "problems." I say "so-called" because spiritual wisdom tells us that problems are opportunities for our growth in disguise. The interesting thing is that if the same problem keeps coming back in our lives, it means that we still haven't learned the underlying inner lesson. Or we have not solved the problem and gone beyond it.

Once I was asked to consult with a restaurant that was having a difficult time. I researched their situation, designed a new way to get feedback from customers, identified "bottlenecks" in their operations, and so on.

It took about a week to "dive" into the situation. Knowing

that an effective solution can be produced through involvement of all the project participants, I brainstormed with the core members of the staff several times. As a result, when I was finalizing a plan to take the restaurant through its crisis, I had the feeling of flight. And this was indeed genuine flight! My role ended at this point. Imagine my disappointment when, six months later, I came to learn that the restaurant was still in crisis. They were never able to find a manager whom the employees could trust and who could drive their new plan forward.

I have often heard directors of companies talk about the need for self-implementing strong solutions. My experience tells me that this is a myth. However, there can be an exception: If the project or decision addresses the world of desires and is based on profit, this can serve as a self-implementing motive. But if the project has a spiritual foundation and is connected with the manifestation of a divine power, then resistance is guaranteed. It stems from our ignorant human nature and the forces that work through it. If we recall the law of entropy (which I described earlier), spiritually based projects are always associated with a decrease in entropy (chaos) and therefore, by definition, require determined effort if they are to succeed. I'm writing all this to emphasise that it's not enough to simply develop an effective solution to a problem; it is essential to implement this decision and see it through to the end. And, because people are the most important part of a project, it is necessary to concentrate fully on deciding who will take responsibility for what tasks.

In conclusion, I would like to share a discovery that helps me to recognise when I have made a correct decision. Every time I am on the right track, and I come to the right decision, I feel a huge relief. The feeling of pressure leaves me and I have a sense of joy. So, to me, this serves as a very reliable compass.

CRISIS MANAGEMENT

No Problem Is Given to Us
That Is Beyond Our Strength

IN THIS CHAPTER I would like to discuss crisis management. This term is most often applied to companies that find themselves on the verge of bankruptcy. The typical approach to this situation involves bringing in analysts, restructuring, making forecasts, changing management and so on. But almost everyone is faced with a crisis at one point or another in their life. We might give it a different name—such as finding our way out of a difficult situation, etc. We will return to this later.

I would like to refer to a saying by Sri Chinmoy:

"For a project to be successful, two things are necessary: Grace from Above and proper management."

This defines the sources of bottlenecks in human activity.

Not all of our activities and projects are necessarily Grace from Above. This is particularly the case when efforts are aimed exclusively at material profit. Life and time correct our activities in the Earth-arena. Taking this point of view, we can see that it's not possible to save every project and activity from failure, no matter how well we manage them. Generally, we need to have enough inner receptivity and intuition to understand the source of a crisis. This is one of the reasons that crisis management companies cannot guarantee a successful result all the time. Part of the problem stems from our human understanding of success. Let's take a closer look:

Take both victory and failure

As parallel experience rivers

Leading to the sea

Of progress-delight.

~ Sri Chinmoy[15]

I can't resist repeating another amazing aphorism by Sri Chinmoy, which opens us to the Grace from Above:

Whatever you are doing,

If you can feel oneness

With other human beings,

With the world,

Then you will be successful

Far beyond your own imagination.

~ Sri Chinmoy[5]

Next, let's assume that everything is all right as far as receiving Grace. Difficult situations can still occur. This is because overcoming difficulties is a good way to make inner progress.

Any approach to getting out of a difficult situation begins with an analysis. We can call this, "Where are we now?" I have had the opportunity to participate in audits of companies several times, and each time, the analysis has been based on a comparison with an ideal model. In the field of software de-

velopment companies we use the Capability Maturity Model Integration (CMMI). In other areas there are ISO standards and other measures that help to define an ideal model. Each of these models has its own advantages and disadvantages, but the approach to the analysis is the same: We need to know what we are looking for, what kind of organisation we want to build. At first it is necessary to draw a comparison with that ideal model in order to understand where our weaknesses are. Despite the variety of human activity, the problems at the entry level are very similar everywhere:

- Insufficient attention to flexible requirements management
- Poor planning and monitoring
- Insufficient or unplanned training
- Weak team spirit (in large companies there is the danger of neglecting a bright individual because of the need to follow procedures and schemas)
- and so on

But when an audit is carried out using only checklists and questionnaires, without using the inner capabilities, it will not be possible to gather accurate information about the underlying causes of the crisis. What is needed is the ability to create a sense of security, to have insight, intuition and a positive approach, and to understand the big picture. Once again we find it necessary to develop our inner qualities and strengths.

I would like to discuss my personal approach to solving difficult situations in my life. After all, in companies, teams and projects, the people involved are the most important contributors. If team members or employees don't have the ability to cope with their own difficulties, this will limit the extent of the solution that can be found.

Every problem has two sides, the undivine, earth-bound side, and the divine side. The first is trying to lead us into a dead end and convince us that "There is no escape. This is the end." The second seeks to bring to the fore our inner strength so that we can succeed in the battlefield of life. It's always important to remember that no problem is given to us that is beyond our capacity to deal with.

Thus, a deeper, esoteric approach tells us that the solution to every problem takes birth in silence. The deeper we can dive into the silence of our mind, the clearer and more natural the solution will be. This is especially so because the mind is not in a position to embrace the entire picture of what is happening. It keeps clinging to details. The resultant anxious and chaotic state restricts us to the surface of life, where we see only the consequences of events that are taking place for unseen inner reasons. This leads to a decision based solely on appearances, which often requires unnecessary Herculean struggles, enormous material expenditures and mental efforts. Again, I would like to remind you of the exercise on calming the mind (AUM.1).

At this point I would like to make a few bold statements: As long as we do not learn to calm the mind and try to envision solutions during meditation, all our external attempts to cope with a problem will be only partially successful. Spiritual practices exist precisely to elevate humans, who are slaves of today's hard realities, from their knees. These practices can transform us into creators of our loftiest dreams and managers of their full implementation. As long as we just read, talk and discuss, but do not practise, everything remains unchanged. It is like running an endless lap.

I remember my first "battle," in 1995, when I was a consultant on the construction of the Hrazdan Power Plant in Armenia. I was responsible for installing Primavera Project Manage-

ment software and making a project plan. The installation of the package was successful. I created the tasks and workflows for the project and optimized the network schedule. When it was time to print all 1,100 project activities, the program could not see the printer. I reset the drivers, rebooted the system, checked the connectors—nothing. I felt as if I had hit a wall.

None of the external solutions worked, so I took a time-out. I went out into the fresh air, sat on a bench and was mesmerised by the beauty and majesty of Mount Ararat. I gazed at the snow-covered peak above the clouds! It embodied so much strength, power and peace! I spontaneously began to meditate.

When I returned to the office, I was fully confident that the printer could not stand up to my inner power. On the first(!) attempt, the project schedule, which occupied half a wall, was printed out.

Since that experience, I have pointed out repeatedly that, especially when you're doing something very useful and necessary (something that reduces the chaos/entropy in life), machines are prone to go on strike. And when all the usual fixes have failed, there is only one solution: the inner strength that originates in peace...

Here is another example. It was an experience involving a friend of mine, who lives in Europe. His boss, who was very fond of tennis, constantly criticized him. She had every reason imaginable: the graph was designed wrong, the colours in a presentation were incorrect, there was a blot in the title of a report, some materials were delivered after the deadline, and so on. My friend was absolutely miserable. He didn't know how to deal with it, because he liked the job itself but not the boss.

We met with him in New York on Sri Chinmoy's birth anniversary. We came up with the idea to write a note about the situation to Sri Chinmoy. To my friend's surprise, Sri Chinmoy called him almost immediately and asked about the problem. Then he concentrated and said, "Go to your boss's tennis tournament, and every time she misses the ball, whistle and shout as loud as you can."

My friend was a little bit shocked by this advice. But he told himself that he wouldn't be alone in the audience, and that it would be hard to single him out when he expressed his "happiness." He decided to carry out Sri Chinmoy's instructions. When he got back home and went to the tennis tournament, imagine his surprise when he found himself to be the only spectator! Even though there was no escape, he started whistling and shouting. At his first whistle, the boss gave him a dirty look. But he decided to continue to the end—he thought his firing was inevitable. However, the next day, to his great surprise, he was not dismissed. Instead, the boss began to show much more tolerance for his mistakes and oversights.

In conclusion, I would like to point out that a non-standard approach or the ultimate solution often cannot be found in the territory of the mind. But if the solution comes as a flash, an inspiration from the heart or from above, then we have every hope of solving the problem.

Here is a quote from Sri Aurobindo:

"There is something above the intellect which one has to discover, and the intellect should be only an intermediary for the action of that source of true Knowledge." [16]

All that makes us inwardly stronger should be used. Anything that weakens us, we must leave.

DEVELOPING A STRONG CHARACTER

Life Devours Us Because We Have Not Developed Inner Power

Every time I run the 3,100-Mile Race, all the artificial things in my life just disappear. All the masks and roles disappear, and I get in touch with my real life and my true self—or the self that I want to be. As I wrote earlier, it is easy to be effective in theory. We know how to organize a project, how to resolve conflicts and how to overcome a crisis. However, sometimes we cannot put this knowledge into action. Our biggest obstacle, as it turns out, is ourselves. The root of the problem is not that the team did not listen to us, that management had insufficient time or that there was not enough financing. The source of the problem is that we did not have sufficient inner power to draw adequate attention to the situation and to direct the flow of activities in the right direction. What are the qualities that have a significant effect on the successful flow of a project? Classical management theory will produce a long list:

- Professionalism
- Analytical skills
- The ability to motivate the team
- A rapid and flexible response to changing conditions

- The ability to negotiate with the client
- and so forth

I agree with this. As a tree has a trunk from which many branches grow, these qualities also have their origin. And as water nourishes all the branches of a tree, there are some qualities that help the entire being to flourish.

Peace of Mind

"There is no peace in the world today, because there is no peace in the minds of men."
~ U Thant, the third Secretary-General of the United Nations.

I mentioned that peace of mind is essential to have a clear vision of the big picture. Speaking more precisely, if we do not have peace of mind, then we are hopelessly weak, and the outside world simply devours us. On the contrary, with peace of mind—even with an iota of peace, we are able to influence events in our lives and to infuse energy into a project. Peace is inner strength. The Vedas say that the entire universe was born from the silence of peace. The power of peace is one of the main creative energies in our lives.

Sincerity

God created you for only two purposes:
One is to be true to Him
And the other is to be true to yourself.
~ Sri Chinmoy [17]

When we "bend" our principles for the sake of our career in order to increase wealth and comfort, we eclipse our true nature, we become weaker. I'm not suggesting that you should ignore the material world and live in austerity. But everything should be balanced. We should adopt the middle way, the golden mean. With spiritual growth we will gain more clarity. We will realize that this material world is to be used for the manifestation of our soul's divine plan. Each one of us has a divine spark, and with regular spiritual practice it will grow into a flame in our hearts and inspiration in our lives to serve others. Each of us has his or her own mission. In one way or another, this mission is connected with the relief of human suffering. Due to the blindness, ignorance and doubt, primarily self-doubt.

Simplicity

Our mind is extremely fond of complicating things. And it is very proud of it. Often we get the impression that the more life develops, the more complicated and confusing it becomes. The more complex and sophisticated our relationships with customers become, the more difficult it is for us to have moments of happiness in our lives. But perhaps you can remember when something simple gave you a moment of joy or relief. How little is needed for happiness! This is very true. I recall the statement of one philosopher: "Over the centuries, the contributions of the mind to human happiness are immeasurably small." To the complexity and confusion of life created by the mind we can compare the clarity and simplicity of the spiritual heart. Having learned to view and perceive the world and people through the heart, we can see their true nature. And we can experience the delight in the beauty and simplicity of the Creator's Plan. It often happens that the solutions to some of the most complicated situations turn out to be extremely simple.

AUM.9 Exercise to develop purity, simplicity, sincerity and confidence

"Kindly repeat the word 'simplicity' inside your mind, inside your head. In silence, please repeat the word 'simplicity' seven times and concentrate only on this particular area of your head (topmost portion of your head over the Sahasrara Chakra or Crown Chakra.)

"Now kindly repeat 'sincerity' seven times inside the heart, in silence, soulfully. Concentrating on your heart, please repeat the word 'sincerity' silently, seven times.

"Now kindly repeat the word 'purity' inside your navel centre or around the navel. Please repeat the word 'purity' seven times in silence, please, most soulfully.

"Now kindly meditate here on the third eye, on the forehead in between the eyebrows, a little above. Kindly repeat 'surety' here, seven times please, in silence.

"Now, please place your hand here on the top of your head and just say three times, 'I am simple, I am simple, I am simple'.

"Now, please place your hand here on your heart and just say three times, 'I am sincere, I am sincere, I am sincere'..

"Now, please place your hand here on your navel and just say three times, 'I am pure, I am pure, I am pure'.

"Now, please place your hand here on the third eye and just say three times, 'I am sure, I am sure, I am sure."[18]

EFFECTIVE DISCUSSION

WHATEVER FIELD WE WORK IN, we participate in or organise discussions. Since ancient times one head has always been better than two. A while ago I began to ask myself whether this type of meeting is actually effective. And to be honest, in most cases—and in most of the projects in which I have been involved—organized discussions have always been very inefficient when comparing the time spent to the results achieved. Furthermore, there is always the question of the quality of the result. Is the solution creative? Is the recommendation of the meeting the most cost-effective solution? This is not to mention the essential question of whether or not the solution actually works. So I started looking for approaches that would help increase the efficiency of meetings and discussions. In the process I came across many interesting suggestions from the managers of successful projects. I'll start with the classical approach, which many people claim is the most effective format for such meetings. Then we'll talk about deeper questions, such as what is necessary to have a perfect meeting.

Ten Rules to Improve the Efficiency of Meetings

1. Keep an open mind. This is perhaps the most essential prerequisite for effective problem-solving in a group. Do not rush to criticise. Instead, listen and try to understand the speaker's perspective. Ask questions and learn. Group problem solving requires each member to be active, both as a participant and as a listener.

2. Be positive. Nothing kills teamwork as quickly as criticism. Nobody wants to be wrong, especially in front of others. The rule for the group discussions should be that any constructive proposals have the right to be heard.

3. Listen! Without this single rule, all the others are useless. Active listening is like playing volleyball. Only one person can serve at a time, but each team member is needed to keep the ball in play.

4. Separate content from the process. Content and process are two separate but equally important parts of the meeting. First is the content, and second is the process of the meeting itself.

5. Select a leader or facilitator. It is rare that a group can work effectively without a leader. Usually, there is a natural leader who will start to guide the group. The leader should focus on the process of the meeting and not try to dominate the discussion of the content.

6. At the start, come to an agreement on the problems that need to be solved. No problem can be solved efficiently before it is clearly defined.

7. Set goals for both the problems (content) and for the meeting (process). People need to understand what needs to be solved during a meeting. They should also understand the limits on time and resources. The role of leader is crucial in this respect.

8. Focus on the targets. Discussion of too many items is not an optimal approach. Setting clearly defined goals and focusing

the team's attention on them will lead to an effective and efficient solution.

9. Defend your views. To work effectively as a group, each member should have the moral strength to defend his or her convictions. If you have good ideas, let them be known. You can be the one to save the group from failing to reach effective decisions.

10. Consensus wins. The best way of addressing a problem within a group is to achieve a consensus. A consensus can be another way of saying, "I may not agree with you completely, but I'm willing to follow your path." It is better to avoid a vote, which can divide the group. Instead, a search for a constructive solution should lead the group to an impartial consensus.

The Secret of the Declaration of Independence

Now, I would like to go beyond the boundaries of classic project management and touch on the esoteric. I think absolutely everyone would like it if others could understand them without words—or with as few as possible. For me, the ideal discussion is one in which there is a one-pointed desire on the part of all the members of the group to minimize any verbal obstacles. I call this "burning." First of all, there is the burning of the heart. I would like to give a powerful historical example. When representatives of the thirteen North American Colonies met in Philadelphia to write and sign the Declaration of Independence in 1776, they were burning with a Vision. They all prayed together in the Christ Church, which still stands in the city. As a result of their oneness and their burning hearts, the Vision of the United States of America came into being. We can judge the strength of this Vision from the fact that although the

U.S. Constitution was created in 1787, there have been only 27 amendments during the following 200 years. Here I quote from one paragraph of the Declaration of Independence written by Thomas Jefferson:

"We hold these truths to be self-evident, that all men are created equal, that they are endowed by their Creator with certain unalienable Rights, that among these are Life, Liberty and the pursuit of Happiness."

Our Mission

I was lucky enough to participate in this kind of discussion, when my closest friends and I were burning with a similar Vision. I also remember the most effective meeting we had, when we shared our common Vision and readily found solutions to the problems we faced. Our own Vision was not associated with seeking a material profit. Service to others was the main goal. (I have already mentioned one of these projects in "The Team" chapter). It seems to me that this kind of motivation for our outer activities is the mission of every individual. But when we discuss business projects, for some reason, it is difficult to use the spiritual heart. When talking about business we find ourselves restricted to the mental plane, with its misunderstandings and divisions. When we cover up our true nature—efficiency is lost.

It is very important that the people involved in a project are, at the very least, like-minded. And it can be a great benefit if they share a common spiritual foundation.

NON-VIOLENT COMMUNICATION

Communication and Understanding in the Leadership Process

I WOULD LIKE TO TURN NOW to the issue of communication and understanding in the leadership process.

As I have said before, people are the key players in every project. As a result, many of the approaches and methods in project management revolve around the issues of how to inspire a person to participate in a project, how to understand his or her interests and how they apply to the project, as well as ways to overcome conflicts and misunderstanding. I am sure you have come across people who do not understand you fully or who do not share your views on a project. I think we all often find that the real motives and aspirations of others remain hidden from us, too. Until we can develop our inner vision with the help of spiritual practices, the veil separating us from others will always be there.

I would like to stress a two-dimensional approach in dealing with any problem. There is the outer technique and there is also the inner content. They are equally important. This is also applicable to communications. If we have inner vision and can understand other people's feelings, we won't need to rely so much on outer techniques. But how often are we able to feel with the heart and not rely on the reasoning mind? At those times when it's difficult to dive deep within during debates and active discussions with other people, the following exercises can be very important. Every time we do these exercises, they stimulate us to look at a problem more deeply and holistically.

Atmatyagi Andrew Kutt, my friend from Washington DC, has directed the Oneness-Family School for many years. They use the Montessori approach. I was amazed to see children of five or six years of age learning academic subjects along with self-discovery, personal development and an awareness of the need to contribute to the development of the world. I quote below the introduction to his lectures, and some of the exercises.

Atmatyagi Andrew Kutt

I've been using the phrases "leadership" and "to be a leader." Here are some of the basics of non-violent communication. Communication is an extremely important element in leadership, and, at the same time, it is a very vast field. It has many different aspects and skills you can learn. But non-violent communication is about listening from your heart and talking about what your needs are. It can also be called compassionate communication. In workshops on non-violent communication, they teach you that any time there are arguments, any time there is miscommunication, there is a reason. And the reason is that someone's needs are not being met and, at the same time, the participants don't understand one another's needs. I have already added this concept to my leadership training. But I can do a future workshop on non-violent communication.

AUM.10 Exercise on Non-violent Communication Number One

In the first few activities you will work with a partner, so please choose one now. In the first activity, both of you will talk for two minutes about something you have done for which you would like to be forgiven, or something you would like to forgive someone else for. It doesn't have to be anybody in the room. It doesn't have to be anybody here today. Simply share something that you would like to forgive in someone else or something that you would like to be forgiven for. The word "forgive" means to let it go from your soul, to surrender it to the Supreme.

You are going to talk for two minutes, and your partner's only job is to listen. There should be no commentary or suggestions; just listening. After two minutes, I will ring a bell and you will exchange roles. Now the one who was talking will listen, and the other person will talk about his or her forgiveness for two minutes. This is the first part of the exercise. After this, the entire group of twenty people will talk for five minutes informally about this forgiveness experience and how it felt.

In the five-minute discussions, each team of twenty should appoint a leader to guide the session. These discussions should be very informal. No one has to speak if they don't want to. It should consist of very gentle sharing. In this way you will learn to feel comfortable expressing the way this activity is making you feel and what you are learning.

AUM.11 Exercise on Non-violent Communication Number Two

We will choose a different partner for exercise number two. In this activity you will talk for three minutes about an experience you had when you made a judgment or an assessment about a situation or a person that was incorrect. After you made your decision, it turned out that you were wrong. From time to time, the partner who is listening will repeat what he or she understood the other partner to have said. You will try to repeat what you have heard—not everything—but some of the key phrases the first person used.

After three minutes the bell will ring, and that is time to switch. The person who was talking before will listen, and the one who was listening will share an experience in which he or she made an incorrect judgement.

There is an important reason for this exercise. To be a good leader, you have to be highly aware of they way you yourself react to situations. This activity is the starting point for learning to master your reactions to events. If you react to situations unconsciously, you will have many problems and find it hard to make progress. If you can control the way you react to events, you can choose consciously how you respond to developments. If we can all develop this ability, then we will have more power and can accomplish greater things.

After this second activity, again join with the same group of

twenty people and the same leader as before. For five to seven minutes talk about this activity and share what you learned from it and what you felt about it.

INSPIRATION

Each Person Comes into the World with the Message of Perfection

UNLESS WE HAVE INSPIRATION, we do everything mechanically. When we operate mechanically, our work is of the worst quality and it takes the longest amount of time to complete it. But when we are burning with enthusiasm and are deeply inspired, the end result is much better and the task is completed much faster. In this connection, I would like to share some words of inspiration from the book Wings of Joy by Sri Chinmoy[15]. I hope it will put you in a good mood and give you a fresh supply of dynamism and enthusiasm!

> *True inner joy is self-created.*
> *It does not depend on outer circumstances.*
>
> *A river is flowing in and through you carrying the message of joy.*
> *This divine joy is the sole purpose of life.*

Be happy!
You will get what you like most.
You will be what you like best.

Remain cheerful,
For nothing destructive can pierce through
The solid wall of cheerfulness.

Be sincere in your thoughts,
Be pure in your feelings.
You will not have to run after happiness.
Happiness will run after you.

I meditate
So that I can inundate
My entire being
With the omnipotent power of peace.

My ego talks,
my humility acts.

If we feel secure
In the depths of our heart,
We shall not challenge anybody,
For inner confidence
Is nothing short of
Complete satisfaction.

Deepen your faith in yourself.
Nothing will be able
To frighten or weaken you.

Yesterday I was clever,
That is why I wanted to change the world.
Today I am wise,
That is why I am changing myself.

Daring enthusiasm and abiding cheerfulness
Can accomplish everything on earth
Without fail.

When the power of love
Replaces the love of power,
Man will have a new name: God.

DEVELOPING VISUALISATIONS

Invincible Weapon in Life

Many of us realise what exceptional strength visualisation has. Perhaps you have watched the movie The Secret. You might have noticed also that being afraid and worrying that you will make a mistake actually make it more likely. Perhaps this happens because every person on earth suffers from self-doubt and worries that he or she will not be able to accomplish something. Of course, this is a universal problem, one that we will come back to. Less common is the "correct" approach to visualisation, when you consciously inject a positive force into a situation or project.

I wrote about the use of visualisation in the chapter on Risk Management. If there are risks that cannot be minimised through ordinary common sense, they can be dealt with by the power of visualisation. I would like to give one example from one of my projects.

At the Height

For several years in the 1990s, my friends and I were working on a project to add Ukraine to the list of countries in the

Sri Chinmoy Peace-Blossoms Nations. This program encourages promoting the ideals of harmony, peace and humane values in a country. More than 30 countries had already joined this project when we began. The countries all signed a declaration that expressed very high aspirations. In some countries the Ministers or MPs signed, and in others it was a group of prominent public figures—even cosmonauts!

But in Ukraine we could not get past the bureaucratic barrier in the Presidential Administration and elsewhere in the government. Eventually, our team hit a dead end. We got to the point where we had no idea who else we could approach to sign the declaration. Coincidentally, in the summer of 1998, most members of the team working on the Peace Nation project, including myself, were participating in the "Oneness-Home Peace Run" in Ukraine. Our route took us over Goverla, the highest mountain in Ukraine. And there, on the highest point in our country, we held hands and imagined that the declaration had already been signed, and that Ukraine had become a Peace-Blossoms Nation. We even said it aloud a few times, "Ukraine is a Peace Nation." Then, the Peace Run journey took us further…

In September, two members of our team both had the idea of meeting with the newly appointed Ukrainian Minister of Sports, who was a former basketball star. I called the Ministry and, to my surprise, I was invited to meet the Minister that same afternoon. We were received very warmly, and the meeting went extremely well. After we had shown the Minister our materials and told many inspiring stories, the Minister asked, "Do I need to sign something?" So on 8 September 1998, thanks to Minister of Sports, Alexander Volkov, Ukraine became the 33rd country to join the Sri Chinmoy Peace-Blossoms Nation project.

AUM.12 Exercise to Develop Visualisation

Now, I would like to explain how to develop imagination and visualisation. In my training courses, I try to present a unique approach to developing strong qualities through identification. Every object or phenomenon in nature embodies one particular quality more than any other. Meditating on an object or phenomenon—in other words, by identifying with it through the spiritual heart—we can absorb its essence surprisingly quickly. For example, the setting sun embodies peace in boundless measure. So, in order to bring peace into our lives and clarity into our mind, we can meditate on a sunset.

Similarly, in order to develop the power of imagination, you could meditate on the full moon[19]. To create a connection with the moon, you should feel that there is a thread stretching from your spiritual heart to the moon. Try to breathe in unison with the moon through this link. Once you have established this link, try to envision the moon in your heart, or enter into it to become the moon itself. This is real identification.

Secrets of The "Secrets"

Using visualisation to resolve problematic or difficult aspects of our projects is no secret. But it doesn't work in some cases. The reason it doesn't work is not dependent on the ability of the individuals or teams concerned. There is a secret about visualisation that not too many people know about.

Our visualisations, like our aspiration, work fully only when they are in resonance with the Will of God. In fact, there is nothing that cannot be achieved or created if it is sanctioned from Above. Allow me to remind you of the amazing statement that I quoted in the section on Crisis Management:

For a project to be successful we need two things: Grace from Above and proper management.

In my opinion, the problem that most people have when they hear about somebody else's will-power—even that of the Supreme—is that it is always perceived as a limitation on their lives. But surprisingly, if we take our mind's will as the only guide, we become more confused, have more doubts and limit ourselves more. At the same time, we become more unhappy.

In more than 23 years practicing meditation, I can confidently say that every time I asked for the fulfilment of the Will from Above in my efforts, I was overwhelmingly happy. This has been the case even if the result did not meet my mind's expectations. But I have never had this feeling of flight and freedom in projects where I was busy executing solutions and expressing my will solely on the basis of my reasoning mind...

WHERE DREAMS COME TRUE

The Fulness of Life

As I usually say during my training courses on Esoteric Project Management, the 3,100-Mile Race is not directly connected with the workshops. But it is strongly connected with myself. I always stress that knowledge and intellectual capacities are not everything, although they are quite necessary in our modern world. But almost everything depends on the character of a person, on his or her qualities. I welcome everything that makes us stronger and that enables us to reveal and manifest our good qualities with an open heart. This is the role the Self-Transcendence 3,100-Mile Race plays in my life. It gives me feelings of flight, freedom and an enormous amount of energy from Above. These feelings flow in and through me and inspire me time and again to accept the challenge and to be there for the start of the Big Race. The Race inspires me and helps me to conquer my weaknesses, my limitations, my doubts and so forth. For me this Race is where my dreams come true.

I would like to share some memories of the race that I have compiled from a number of interviews over the years.

3,100 Miles, 50 Days and 16 Pairs of Running Shoes

3,100 miles in 50 days is a challenge for the strong and those who know nothing is impossible. Stutisheel Oleg Lebedev is among the few who take part in the world's longest certified footrace. In 2004, he became the first person from the CIS to complete the distance. The Self-Transcendence 3,100-Mile Race takes place annually from mid-June to early August in Jamaica, Queens, New York. Read his interview about finding the energy and strength to cover an ultra-marathon distance.

When did the 3,100 Mile Race become more than a hobby for you?

It's hard to say, because my entire conscious life was about sports, starting with cross-country skiing when I was a child. I ran my first marathon in 1994. That was the starting point that opened the door to long-distance races. By then I had recognized that a large part of my life revolved around running. I have participated in the 3,100-Mile Race ten straight times. So it is much more than a hobby for me.

Have you ever won it?

My best finish so far has been fifth place. But the 2011 race was won by Sarvagata Mikhail Ukrainski, who used my lectures and books as part of his training. So, I'm proud to have made a contribution to his victory as well. But, in fact, those of us who run the race noticed a long time ago that the place we finish doesn't matter that much. We don't look at the results very often. The most important aspect of the race is what happens while we're running—managing the difficulties, supporting the others or not, and so on. One time a journalist who came to the

race every day asked each runner, "How many miles have you run so far?" The significant thing was that no one could answer correctly. The one fact everyone knew was the number of laps they had done so far that day.

How many people take part in the Big Race?

The number of participants is between ten and fourteen people. The year that had the most runners was 2007, when there were fifteen people. They come from all different countries, Ukraine, Russia, Germany, Slovakia, Australia, Switzerland, USA, Canada and others. In 2014, there were twelve participants from eight countries, including three women.

What is the ordinary routine for a runner during the race?

Every day we start at 6:00 am. I get up at 5:10 am. That leaves me 30-40 minutes to get ready. In the morning, to prepare myself for the day ahead, I spend 5-10 minutes meditating. Then helpers drive us to the race, and we're at the starting line by 5:50 am. At 6:00 am we begin our "workday," which lasts eighteen hours. The course is open from 6:00 am to midnight. Every day we try to do our best. Once we start, anything that happened yesterday or the day before doesn't matter at all. Every day you start this race anew. Our life is divided into laps. We don't know how many laps we have run overall, but we know exactly how many we have completed each day. On an average day I run about 120 laps— around 65 miles. Each lap is 0.548 mi. On a difficult day I have to be satisfied with 90-100 laps. But that's still quite far—about 50 mi.

The first year I ran the race, I realized very quickly I had to find my own style, rhythm and pace. When I was a novice, I watched the other runners: who had breaks and when, when they took their vitamins, and so on. I was able to absorb some of the things the veterans did, for example, how to adjust my running shoes or how my shoelaces should be tied. But the most important thing is to find your own pace—one that is comfortable and that you can keep up for a long time. I found that taking fifteen-minute breaks is perfect for me. Fifteen minutes is long enough to give you a rest but not so long that the body gets a chance to cool down. We sleep during these short breaks. Over the past years I have gotten so comfortable with this that I even manage to have dreams. Then, when the alarm goes off you return as if from "a galaxy far, far away" back to the race.

I have never seen a better time-management course than the one you get at this race. The runners have to learn to optimize their time expenditure and to save every second. The race is long, and all aspects of it are interconnected. If one day you spend ten or fifteen minutes longer at the race, it means you go to bed ten to fifteen minutes later, accordingly. Then you get less sleep. The entire ultra-marathon is like one indivisible flow. In our daily life we divide months into weeks and weeks into days. We know that, for example, we can sleep late on the weekend. But I find that, with the right attitude, mood and perception, only five hours of sleep a night is enough. I take only two or three short breaks during the day, and that is also enough.

Do you have breakfast/lunch/dinner breaks during the day?

For the past four to five years we have had a devoted team of volunteer cooks who take 50 days of unpaid leave to work at the race. They bring hot food to the race three times a day. We eat very small portions while walking through the camp. I ask the helpers to put my food in small plastic cups, and before each lap I eat one cup and start running again. Eaten this way, breakfast can last several hours. And right after that is lunch. So

we eat about 50 times a day. And still we lose weight.

What are you thinking about while running?

Well, the mind is quite calm during the race. There is a direct correlation between intense physical training and peace of mind. The mind becomes peaceful while running. By nature I am a rather calm person, but during this race I can't help but enjoy my inner peace. Focusing on one single thing can be rather difficult in ordinary life. But during the race it's quite easy. I listen to music ninety percent of the time. But it's not the kind of music I listen to normally that helps me during the 3,100. Over time I have developed a strong liking for Indian music, with its spontaneity and natural flow. It fits free running perfectly. It is simply amazing.

And do you think about work?

No, I definitely do not think about work. Once I start, my workaday world drops away very quickly. During the race my life revolves around running. Of course, my work makes the race possible financially. In my work I try to take on interesting projects. I work on developing processes in projects using CMMI and Agile methods. The projects I work on are ones I'm interested in. I look for varied development opportunities. I'm also very interested in taking training courses. And in addition to this, I receive a salary, most of which is used to finance my trips to competitions. So, both parts of my life work together. I have never made it a secret that participating in these extreme events is the number one priority in my life. Because of this, I have to find a new job more often than otherwise, approximately every other year.

Do you notice what is happening around you while running?

Yes, you see everything, and you're aware of a whole range of things. The most attentive runners collect the coins, mp3 players and cell phones on the road. One runner has found five cell phones in seven years of running the race. I like to look up. Of course, the runners have to look down to see where they're going, but I've always been attracted to the sky. I like looking at it very much, and I also like to fly. I have never seen anything like the sky at the 3,100-Mile Race. Since New York is on the ocean, the weather can be very variable. The sky is never the same from one day to the next. You see fantastic sunrises, breathtaking sunsets and bright rainbows across the whole sky. They create the most memorable impressions. Also, in the U.S. you can often see skywriting. This is a type of advertisement created by several airplanes using special smoke to write letters in the sky to produce messages. It is very funny to watch.

How many pairs of sneakers wear out per season?

Sixteen pairs per race. Taking into account the fact that the average pair of sneakers costs $75-80, it's not cheap.

Aside from having to change your jobs frequently, what other cons does your hobby have?

I wouldn't say that having to find a new job is a negative thing. On the contrary, each new job provides an impetus for further development. It is actually an advantage for me. I am confident that there are things in life that spur development without any side effects. This race, which was founded by Sri Chinmoy, a spiritual master, is much more profound than it appears. For many runners–including myself–it is a spiritual pilgrimage. This is why it is so important for me. It is not a mere competition where I win a place–I never think about that stuff.

First and foremost are my experience, my progress, my spiritual development and service to mankind. After my first race in 2004, I got an inner inspiration to offer training courses and give lectures on the 3,100-Mile Race. Since that time, thousands of people from the different post-Soviet countries have participated in my courses and attended my lectures. I see people getting interested in and carried away by the incredible distances we cover. But after that, the question of how it can be done comes up. The answer is in the inner dimension—when you see the world with your heart and you get energy from within.

Certainly, there are people who look askance at your hobby, aren't there?

There surely are. When I first started giving lectures, I didn't have any videos from the race. I would start my talk, and athletes from the front rows would stand up and leave. They thought it was all lies! There are still people who give me puzzled looks. They cannot understand why a person would spend all his money, not on making himself comfortable, but on having near-death experiences during an exhausting race abroad. But I am driven by those who are inspired.

Have you ever felt like quitting it all and lying idly on the beach?

Essentially, I am calm, but very active. I can endure only a day or two at the beach. To me, resting is running, riding a bike, paddling a kayak or parachuting – the more exciting, the better. Thus far I have parachuted five times. It's an unforgettable experience. Clearly, over the years there have been several difficult moments during the 3,100. In all my ten years of participation there were two years–2009 and 2014–when I ran the entire ultra-marathon as if I was powered by a nuclear reactor. I set my personal best of 48 days +03 hours 57 minutes and 19 seconds (64.4 mi/day) in 2014. Out of those 48 days, only three were difficult. The race seemed to go by very quickly. Of the ten races I started, I finished eight. Once I didn't finish due to a knee injury, and the second time I didn't meet the time cutoff. So, there have been many different experiences in my sports life. But quitting completely never occurred to me. Maybe it's because I feel that I'm destined to do this race. No one can say it's easy to run 3,100 miles. But the great thing is that a person can do it. Perhaps I have an inner core that helps me master this kind of effort.

From where do you draw energy and strength?

People ask me two questions almost always: Why do you do this? Where do you get the strength? As for why I do it, I can say it's part of my mission in life. It was a dream that I first had in 2004. Until that time I had never known that I wanted to run the world's longest race. From where do I draw strength? The strength comes from within. More specifically, meditation helps me a lot. There's an aphorism by Sri Chinmoy that helps me orientate myself and distribute my strength properly: "A happy heart increases the speed of the body." When you feel happy inside, when you are in a positive mood, you run much more easily and faster. A positive mood is one of the secrets of how to run the 3,100-Mile Race. The race is much easier to complete when you're happy, instead of checking your watch all the time and trying to meet some set milestones.

Do you have an ultimate goal?

My answer will be another of Sri Chinmoy's aphorisms: "Today's finish is just tomorrow's starting point."

SPENDING MONEY PROPERLY

AT EVERY MOMENT we receive proposals about how to make money. And, in fact, the greater part of our lives revolves around this goal. Classic project management seeks to achieve the same goal: to generate the expected revenue from a project in a given time and with a certain investment. Entire systems and approaches to management are based on successful projects, best practices and knowledge bases. But we rarely think that making money is only one side of the coin. To complete the picture we must consider the subsequent spending of this money. In fact, earning and spending are related. I am not afraid to call this a cosmic law:

How we spend money is directly related to how we earn it.

It's not the other way around, as you might have thought! This law is valid from our personal lives to the scale of the Earth itself. But I don't want to talk about "rocket science." I will confine myself to the personal scale. Like it or not, all countries, all mega-organisations, are made up of people. The culture and level of consciousness of each individual determine the level of action of the larger organisations. So let's start with ourselves. It is extremely rare to find training courses on how to spend money properly. I have never found one. At best, this sort of course teaches how to invest and increase your profits.

However, a major driving force and motivation for us to spend money exists in the background. It can be briefly described as "more comfort." All selling is aimed at fulfilling this desire. And, as we know, no desire comes by itself. It is good that there is Someone who adjusts or, I would say, enlightens our desires and leads us periodically to the difficult situation in which there is little or no money.

It is remarkable that there are universal laws that govern our desires, and that we often face critical situations that force us to ask important questions like "Why does everything around me exist? Why am I here on Earth?" I have discussed this issue many times. In addition to the deeper questions related to self-knowledge and self-expression, I firmly believe that we live to serve others. We live to help other people reach a new level of life, where the positive approaches of honesty, understanding, respect, tolerance, and many other good qualities will be the norm rather than the exception.

If we return to Maslow's hierarchy (which was discussed earlier), at the primary level each person is motivated to fill his or her basic needs for housing, food, clothing and so on. So that is where money is spent. But this is only the INITIAL LEVEL. If we get stuck at that level, we will continue to strive to earn more and spend more for a more comfortable life. Then we will begin to experience the inevitable consequences of the universal laws: depression, misery, disease, dissatisfaction with life and so on. These laws are actually designed to force us to look deeper into our lives, our goals and our ideals.

We can translate these laws into practical language:

To receive twice as much, we need to properly spend twice as much.

To spend properly, you must involve your heart and soul.

It must be done with dedication and selflessness. This means that you have to seek a higher goal than just making life comfortable. Here are a few examples of projects that I have found interesting and into which I have invested:

- The Oneness-Heart-Tears and Smiles humanitarian projects
- The Oneness-Home Peace Run, an international torch relay
- Self-Transcendence Races, in particular the Ukrainian national championships for 24H and 48H
- Lectures and workshops on healthy lifestyles and meditation
- Concerts of meditation music

I have seen again and again that these projects have very high goals and ideals. Because of this they attract all the resources necessary: the right people, effective meetings, development of essential skills, adequate financing and so on. We should treat money as just a tool. We really need wisdom and guidance from Above to make and spend money wisely. There are an infinite number of examples of how spending money wrongly or desiring for material wealth without striving for spiritual wealth or without pure thoughts have resulted in anxiety, depression, frustration and even decline, not only for individuals, but for entire countries.

I would like to refer to some profound thoughts about motivation from Mother Teresa. Perhaps this is the best possible way to answer the question, "What is it all about?"

Do It Anyway

People are often unreasonable, irrational, and self-centered. Forgive them anyway.

If you are kind, people may accuse you of selfish, ulterior motives. Be kind anyway.

If you are successful, you will win some unfaithful friends and some genuine enemies. Succeed anyway.

If you are honest and sincere, people may deceive you. Be honest and sincere anyway.

What you spend years creating, others could destroy overnight. Create anyway.

If you find serenity and happiness, some may be jealous. Be happy anyway.

The good you do today will often be forgotten. Do good anyway.

Give the best you have, and it will never be enough. Give your best anyway.

In the final analysis, it is between you and God. It was never between you and them anyway."

~Mother Teresa

PROJECT NUMBER ONE

Our Life

I WOULD LIKE TO FOCUS on most important project for all of us: the project of our life. While working, making our home comfortable, solving daily problems and misfortunes, we sometimes find ourselves drowning in the minor details of life. When this happens, we have lost—or perhaps never even found—the integral picture, the Vision, the Dream of our life. Let us remember that we came to this earth with a mission; you can call it Role, Purpose or Goal. Why is it that, year after year, we are not getting any closer to our dreams and goals? Why does the same pattern keep repeating itself day after day, as we spend most of our time on secondary issues, on the hustle and bustle of life? We find that we have neither time nor energy for the most important things. In one of my training courses a participant said that health might be the first indicator of how successfully we are pursuing our dreams and our mission. So we can see that unusual health problems quite often indicate internal distortions in one's attitude to life, or the presence of artificial priorities.

The Parable of the Priorities

One time a philosopher was giving a lecture on priorities in life. He took an empty jar and filled it with rocks.

Is the jar full?
Yes, it's full.

Then he took some pebbles, and poured them into the jar between the stones, filling it up.

Is the jar full?
Yes, it's full.

Then he poured sand into the jar, filling the remaining spaces.

Is the jar full?
Yes, it's full.

He then filled the jar to the brim with water. Once again, the jar was full.

It is the same in our own lives. The stones represent the primary issues, our base. Then come the minor concerns, the pebbles, for which we also spend time and energy. Everything else is represented by the sand and water.

But be careful not to do it in reverse. If you fill the jar with sand and water first, the pebbles and the large stones will not fit.

I intentionally called this book *Esoteric Project Management*, rather than *Esoteric Business Management*. The objectives are different, as are the priorities. I wanted to emphasise the role of material goals and their secondary importance.

But coming back to Project Number One, in order to evaluate our progress toward our dreams, we just have to see how much time every day we devote to their fulfilment. This picture might not be so inspiring.

What is the solution to this situation?

I would like to share what works for me. The more general and deeper answer is: aspiration. There are two items that will help us start (and continue)

1. Physical activities
2. The practice of calming the mind

Humanity was created for movement. But many of us, catastrophically, lack any movement. There is a secret: Physical activity clears the mind. Sri Chinmoy taught that we are able to increase the receptivity of our system through physical exertion.

I remember an incident that occurred during my schooldays. The day was very difficult. There were problems with my teachers. I had a lot of homework. Then some tension occurred with my parents. Everything hit at the same time. I was almost in tears when I went to my regular cross-country ski training. But gradually, with physical exertion, all the frightening pressure subsided. It left my mind first. And by the time I got home, pretty much exhausted, I was in a good mood and had a clear idea about how to deal with my problems. I decided to solve them one after the other, slowly and deliberately.

If you start exercising regularly, you will see how your life-problems clear up and how the pressure of time just disappears. It has to be the kind of exercise that works up a sweat, like running, biking, swimming and so on. For beginners, I recommend a formula of three days of training and one day of rest. I use this schedule myself when I'm trying to get in shape.

The vast majority of people have chaotic thoughts in their minds. In most cases, the external environment in which we spend the day only increases this "mess." For a fruitful life, to be able to act consciously with clarity and peace of mind is absolutely necessary. Peace of mind fulfils our life.

"Without peace the outer world is not only wicked to the backbone, but also hopelessly weak. A wicked world has tremendous energy. Unfortunately, its energy is directed towards a false goal, a goalless shore." [20]

Please refer once again to the exercise for calming the mind—AUM.1

When we are progressing towards the destination of our dreams, we feel joy in our heart. This joy can overwhelm us and give our life fullness and meaning. This state of happiness is not dependent on external circumstances—even if we do not achieve what we were hoping for. Deep joy comes from right action, from movement in the right direction. And rest assured, "corrections" come from Above much faster when we are in motion. In fact, the first thing we have to do is to clarify our Vision for our most important project. Without a coherent Vision of our life, its purpose and role, all the methods of project management, organisation, motivation and time management lose their importance and significance.

Around fifteen years ago, at a workshop, we were requested to meditate on our Goal. And since it was a gathering of friends, we wrote the result on a large sheet of paper at the front of the room. During the whole exercise, one thought was constantly spinning through my head: the culture of project management. I stood up to write this down. But ... as I walked to the stage, I got a glimpse ... And I wrote a totally different subject—my most important project. The culture of project management turned out to be only the tool. But was a good thought anyway...

MANTRAS IN ACTION

The Eastern Approach to Achieving Prosperity and Health

THE QUALITIES OF THE EAST and the West are well known. The former turns inward to find inspiration, enlightenment and strength. The latter is active, sometimes tearing down walls to achieve its goal. By synthesizing these two approaches we can reach a whole new level.

Today, however, I would like to focus on the Eastern approach. There are already enough books on action. The fact is that the Hindu tradition has deities who foster different areas of human activity. For example, the goddess Saraswati is the patron of the arts. The classic Hindu approach to solving problems lies in pleasing the appropriate deity. Perhaps this idea makes you smile. But even in our day-to-day world, to cope with a challenge, we try to get a meeting with the boss, not the subordinates. For example, if we take the Eastern approach to solving financial problems, it is necessary to please the goddess of fortune. In India, since ancient times, different mantras have been chanted to please each deity. And if the deities were satisfied with the sincerity and spirituality of the aspirant, the gods and goddesses would appear and fulfil their every desire. Here is the ancient Sanskrit money mantra. If you take it seriously, you can obtain financial help. Sri Chinmoy gave this mantra to one of his disciples who had financial problems, and after thirteen days of reciting the mantra her finances improved tremendously.

AUM.13 The Money Mantra

Ya Devi sarvabhutesu

Ratna rupena sangstitha

Nastasvai namastasvai

Namastasvai namo namah

I bow and bow and again. I bow to the Supreme Goddess who resides in all human beings in the form of material wealth and prosperity.[21]

But it is good to remember that if you do not have faith in the mantra, or you do it mechanically, you will never get results. This applies not only to mantras.

Our Health - The Start of Management

To begin with, I would like to bring renowned thoughts of Voland from The Master and Margarita by Mikhail Bulgakov:

"...in order to govern, one needs, after all, to have a precise plan for a certain, at least somewhat decent, length of time. Allow me to ask you, then, how can man govern, if he is not only deprived of the opportunity of making a plan for at least some ridiculously short period, well, say, a thousand years, but cannot even vouch for his own tomorrow? And in fact,—here the stranger turned to Berlioz—imagine that you, for instance, start governing, giving orders to others and yourself, generally, so to speak, acquire a taste for it, and suddenly you get ...hem ... hem ... lung cancer ... —here the foreigner smiled sweetly, and if the thought of lung cancer gave him pleasure—yes, cancer—narrowing his eyes like a cat, he repeated the sonorous word—and so your governing is over! You are no longer interested in anyone's fate but your own. Your family starts lying to you. Feeling that something is wrong, you rush to learned doctors, then to quacks, and sometimes to fortune-tellers as well. Like the first, so the second and third are completely senseless, as you understand. And it all ends tragically: a man who still recently thought he was governing something, suddenly winds up lying motionless in a wooden box, and the people around him, seeing that the man lying there is no longer good for anything, burn him in an oven.

"Yes, man is mortal, but that would be only half the trouble. The worst of it is that he's sometimes unexpectedly mortal—there's the trick! And he cannot even say what he will be doing this evening."

This is the passage from Bulgakov's work that I like the best! That is why all the management theories I recommend start from one's own health. How can you implement management techniques and elegant solutions when you are depressed, tired or have a serious disease?

Recently, I found full versions of the mantras for health and energy. It is noteworthy that I found them in a lecture Sri Chinmoy gave on "Beauty" at the University of Montana in Missouri on 23 April 1974. I have often noticed that when you are full of energy, you have no pain or worries. But when energy is lacking, immediately old injuries and weak parts of the body make themselves felt... So I use these two mantras together. They were created and used by the Vedic seers more than 10,000 years ago. It is amazing that they survived!

"When beauty in the vital dawns, we become energetic, dynamic, progressive and fulfilling. At that time, we pray to the Supreme to inundate our vital with power infinite, power divine, the power that builds, not the power that breaks; the power that energises us, the power the vital needs for the full manifestation of divinity on earth. This power in the vital is the beauty of the vital for the manifestation of God here on earth."[20]

AUM.14 The Energy Mantra

Tejo hasi tejo mayi dhehi

Virjam asi virjam mayi dhehi

Valam asi valam mayi dhehi

Ojo hasi ojo mayi dhehi

Manyur asi manyur mayi dhehi

Saho asi saho mayi dhehi

Thy fiery spirit I invoke.

Thy manly vigour I invoke.

Thy power and energy I invoke.

Thy battle fury I invoke.

Thy conquering mind I invoke..

AUM.15 The Health Mantra

"I also try to invoke the body-consciousness and become one with the aspiring body in order to discover beauty in the body. For this, I pray to the Supreme to grant me sound health and an aspiring body.

Om Tac caksur devahitam purastacchukram uccarat

Pasyema saradah satam

Jivema saradah satam

Smuyama saradah satam

Prabavama saradah satam

Adinah syama saradah satam

Bhuyasca sradah satat

May we, for a hundred autumns, see that lustrous Eye,
God-ordained, arise before us.
May we live for a hundred autumns;
May we hear for a hundred autumns;
May we speak well for a hundred autumns;
May we hold our heads high for a hundred autumns;
Yes, even beyond a hundred autumns.

In this case, a hundred years means an infinite or indefinite expanse of time. If we have a long life of aspiration on earth, then we can realise God, reveal God and manifest God. We need a long life of aspiration, dedication, devotion and surrender. This is the beauty in the body and of the body, for the soul and for God, the Supreme."

As you can see, the greatest secrets of this world are completely available. What is needed is our faith and practice. If these mantras remain unpractised, it is unlikely that they will manifest their ancient mystical power in your life. It all depends on discipline and willpower.

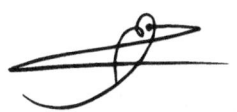

PROPER NUTRITION

Food Can Be Our Friend or Enemy; It's Up to Us

AS ALWAYS, I ADHERE TO A HOLISTIC APPROACH to life. In this book I cannot leave out the important topic of proper nutrition. I would like to emphasize the idea that we operate, manage, talk and make decisions from our present standard. No matter how many wise books we read, whatever correct thoughts we might have, until they become an integral part of our lives we will continue to make mistakes constantly. We will just pretend that we know what we are doing. The standard, or the level of consciousness we have, varies even throughout the day. Bad news can make us depressed, so that we are not able to make decisions. On the contrary, sudden encouragement or an inspirational message can take us to the skies. Then everything in our life becomes miraculously flawless.

I would like to talk about more mundane things. There is the expression, "A healthy mind in a healthy body." There is also another popular expression that fits the subject, "We are what we eat." Scientists established long ago that there is a relationship between one's eating habits and one's mental condition. Nutrition is a good tool, and can be a basis for the improvement of our current standard.

I would like to quote a few excerpts from my book Eat to Run. I am not a doctor or a dietician. But based on my participation in the 3,100-Mile Race, I would like to share my experience. I am sure you will agree, that it is rare that someone runs 60 miles per day for 50 days. Nutrition is part of a general approach to solving this problem.

I Eat No Being

The vast majority of ultramarathon runners are vegetarians. Even those who started out as meat eaters eventually came to prefer a vegetarian diet. I have been a vegetarian for the past 23 years. I do not eat meat or fish. "The Big Race" is the best touchstone for all the theories I discuss here. Likewise, I can state with certainty that the theories about indispensable amino acids or the deficiencies of vegetarian diets do not hold water. During my 23 years of participation in many extreme races, I have rebuilt my body several times. I keep feeling better and better each day. Many websites provide information on how to establish a vegetarian diet.

I would also like to mention some famous vegetarians: Leonardo Da Vinci, Leo Tolstoy, Benjamin Franklin, Arthur Schopenhauer, Mahatma Gandhi, Albert Einstein, Carl Lewis and Muhammad Ali. I would like also to note that strict practitioners of Ayurvedic medicine refuse to treat meat-eaters. This is something to think about.

During the race, I try to follow the most practical approach to eating. I always want to eat less so as to save time. But at the same time, I still want to get more energy. Animal food is not ap-

propriate because of the amount of energy it requires to digest, and its low energy efficiency.

While vegetarianism is very important, it's only the beginning. It's not enough to eliminate animal products from our diet. Everyone should eat a well-balanced diet. This is even more important for athletes who expend large amounts of energy.

During my first race, I hardly knew what I should eat. I was only aware of a few things I had read, together with comments from former participants and what I had heard from several ultramarathon runners I knew. I was surprised that all the doctors at the race recommended that I give up eating sweets like chocolate and sugary desserts. Since then I've learned that during long-term low-level efforts like slow long-distance running, carbohydrates lose their leading status as "fuel" because they are consumed too fast. Indeed, I have often experienced a burst of energy after eating candy only to have it quickly followed by a slump during which I felt even more exhausted than before I ate it.

This continued until I began to explore some approaches I had heard about. I learned that fats comprise the main fuel for multiday races. Proteins are needed for building muscle. One of the pioneers of multi-day races, Trishul Cherns, told me about the Zone Diet, which is composed of 40% carbohydrates, 30% proteins and 30% fats. For example, you can eat rice for carbohydrates; tofu for proteins, and olive oil for fat. Fats that work for me include oil from olives, cashews and avocados, as well as ghee. Some of the other runners drink milk, but I eliminated most dairy products from my diet after I got food poisoning from milk and cheesecake. In addition to this, digestion of any milk products becomes more difficult with age.

The Theory and Practice of Holistic Nutrition

Speaking of a well-balanced diet, I must also mention the holistic approach. The first time I heard about this was from my good friend Abarita Danzer, the owner of the vegetarian food producer Soyana, which is based in Switzerland.

The main idea of holistic nutrition is to preserve the natural integrity of any ingredients, and to avoid products that were not created in nature. Grain is a good example of a natural food. Look at how balanced and complete it is, with its ability to sprout when planted. Grain gives new life and is completely self-sufficient. Not only does it contain all the elements essential for a new plant, it also has them in a perfectly balanced form. Grains are composed of bran, germ, cellulose, vitamins, minerals, proteins, and carbohydrates.

Nevertheless, food manufacturers have decided to improve on natural grains. They split it into different parts. The finest white flour contains only proteins and carbohydrates. This is the part used most in our everyday diet. Some vitamins and minerals remain in coarse dark flour. The most precious parts, the bran and germ are sold for animal feed!

It's hard to imagine how white flour could ever give new life. Not only is it a product of mechanical process, but it is also a mixture of elements that do not exist in nature. This means that white flour can unbalance our system.

During multi-day races, under great extremes of exertion, we reap what we have sown in our style of life. It shows in our performance. As you can see, diet is just the tip of the iceberg. Granted, using a special diet right before the race is important, but what really matter are our everyday habits and nutrition.

After my first few races, I completely cut sugar and white flour from my diet. Imperfect health is too high a price to pay for whatever pleasure can be found in this kind of food.

Honey and stevia are natural sweeteners that are acceptable if necessary. But most herbal teas taste more natural and have more depth without any sweetener at all.

Both during a race and in my everyday life I prefer wholegrain cereals like unpolished rice, barley, oats, and my favourite—buckwheat.

Intuitively, I always understood the benefits of leaving an interval between eating and drinking. The ancient practices of Ayurveda confirm this. It might not be so comfortable during the race; nevertheless it's still possible to wait 10-20 minutes after a meal to drink. When I'm not running, I drink liquids 10-20 minutes before a meal, and again within half an hour after finishing eating.

During the run-up to the 3,100, I don't heavily eat before my morning workout. It is believed that until noon our bodies cleanse themselves of wastes and toxins, and that we should not strain the body by eating a lot before that time. Fruit, herbal tea and fresh juice are fine before noon. Over the years I have gotten used to this regime. Now I don't feel hungry in the morning at all.

Just like everybody else these days, I suffer from a technological bias when natural foods are replaced by processed brands with synthetic additives, which make the products cheaper but not at all healthful. For example in the U.S., most juice brands contain synthetic vitamin C. My body rebels against this additive during a race. I get heartburn or even a rash on my legs and feet.

During training, when I'm stretched for time restrictions, I often have to drink apple or other juices from a local supermarket. But I always pay the price for synthetic additives like flavourings, preservatives, sugar and so on. During the first week of a race, I used to feel as if I had been poisoned. But I knew the truth all those years. It was obvious what damaged me when I compared my reactions to supermarket juice with my reactions to fresh homemade juice, made with my own vegetables and fruit, grown with love and care. It wasn't until 2010 that I refused to drink any store-bought juices, no matter how much time pressure I was under. It just took some time to put my knowledge into practice!

DEVELOPING ENERGY FOR PROJECT IMPLEMENTATION

The Secrets of Making Progress

I WAS IN SINGAPORE when the year 2011 dawned. When I got home, because of jet lag and the long flight, I found myself with virtually no inspiration to do anything. There were quite important projects that needed my attention, but each one looked to be in worse shape than the next. On one project, the client customer wouldn't approve my proposals. On another, there were so many problems that progress seemed impossible. And the third seemed to be stuck in limbo. This doesn't happen to me very often, but when it does, it is usually because of low levels of life-energy. When you feel weak, nothing goes well. The way I felt then, even perfect project management techniques would not help. What I needed was to increase my energy and find some inspiration.

I remembered my best solution to this kind of problem.

If you feel bad or if things aren't going well, put everything out of your mind, lace up your running shoes and go out running for an hour or an hour and a half. You'll feel infinitely happier and you'll find the enthusiasm to get going again.

And that's just what happened! Running through the snowy woods, I felt a surge of strength. And I remembered an aphorism of Sri Chinmoy's that said that energy comes from motion. You know the similar proverb, "A rolling stone gathers no moss."

When I got home after my run, it turned out that the client had approved my proposal, one that would give a strong boost to the project. When I looked at the project about which I had so many negative feelings, my attitude changed because I found information about some other companies that went through the same difficulties. Despite having a hard time during startup they eventually succeeded. After a few phone calls and some newly signed contracts, things cleared up on the third project. Once again I was struck by how much inner power can help clear away obstacles.

If we just follow our human nature, any difficulties can compel us to withdraw, hide or isolate ourselves. And that is just the opposite of what is necessary to restore our life force. We need to move! Putting on your running shoes works every time.

But there is another vector of motion that can help me tremendously in difficult situations. This is self-giving. Below I would like to bring the original text by Sri Chinmoy, which can rightly be called the secret of progress.

The Ten Godly Secrets of Giving and Taking

1. Love is giving without the expectation of receiving anything in return. Taking is getting back that portion of love you have already shared with others.

2. If you would take, you must first learn to give; if you would receive, you must open your heart and share.

3. Give to the world the best you have and the best will fly back to you.

4. The wise man does not store up his treasures. The more he gives to others, the more he has left over for himself.

5. Giving means getting the bread that you cast upon the waters is bread that ultimately comes to you.

6. You can only give what you have in your purse; you can only receive what you have already doled out.

7. Presents and money are not gifts; they are poor substitutes for gifts; the only true gift is that portion of yourself that you have shared with others.

8. When you give something to your brother and your sister, you lose nothing. You gain whenever your brother and sister gain because your brother and sister are your very own Self.

9. God loves the cheerful giver. God loves the anonymous giver. He who gives cheerfully and secretly gives a portion of himself to God.

10. This is the final supreme secret—you only get to keep that which you give away.

MOVING ROCKS

Tasks Beyond Our Strength

ESOTERIC PROJECT MANAGEMENT is associated with attracting forces that have more power than our ordinary human capabilities. Applying power to bottlenecks, decreasing the probability of risk, powerfully motivating the project team and—most importantly—having a Vision for the entire project are all essential. That's why I focus on the development of inner strength and the use of spiritual practices in management. In this chapter, I would like to share a story that I hope will help you cope with any problems that seem to be beyond your strength.

Parable

A little boy was spending his Saturday morning playing in his sandbox. He had with him his box of cars and trucks, his plastic pail, and a shiny, red plastic shovel. In the process of creating roads and tunnels in the soft sand, he discovered a large rock in the middle of the sandbox.

The boy dug around the rock, managing to dislodge it from

the dirt. With a little bit of struggle, he pushed and nudged the rock across the sandbox by using his feet. (He was a very small boy, and the rock was very large.) When the boy got the rock to the edge of the sandbox however, he found that he couldn't roll it up and over the little wall.

Determined, the little boy shoved, pushed, and pried, but every time he thought he had made some progress, the rock tipped and then fell back into the sandbox. The little boy grunted, struggled, pushed and shoved; but his only reward was to have the rock roll back, smashing his chubby fingers.

Finally he burst into tears of frustration. All this time the boy's father watched from his living room window as the drama unfolded. At the moment the tears fell, a large shadow fell across the boy and the sandbox. It was the boy's father. Gently but firmly he said,

"Son, why didn't you use all the strength that you had available?"

Defeated, the boy sobbed back,

"But I did, Daddy, I did! I used all the strength that I had!"

"No, son," corrected the father kindly. "You didn't use all the   strength you had. You didn't ask me."

With that the father reached down, picked up the rock and removed it from the sandbox.

Do you have "rocks" in your life that need to be removed? Are you discovering that you don't have what it takes to lift them? There is One who is always available to us and willing to give us the strength we need. Isn't it funny how we try so hard to do things ourselves.

- Unknown author

Now the question arises, how to ask this One? There are two languages to commune with God: prayer and meditation. I found a very interesting definition given by Sri Chinmoy:

"When we pray, we speak and God listens; when we meditate, we listen and God talks." [22]

The second part is the most interesting. It is precisely the internal messages of meditation that provide guidance and answers. Synthesizing meditation with management techniques could be a very effective way to arrive at our goal.

ACHIEVE THE IMPOSSIBLE!

Advice from Sri Chinmoy

PROBABLY EACH OF US has been faced with a situation in which no management techniques could solve the problem and no one had any idea what would work. In other words, you "hit the wall." This can happen because the project is beyond our ability or completely outside our experience.

When I first read this it completely shocked me, because it was about achieving the impossible. Specifically it talked about breaking the two-hour barrier in the marathon (26.2 mi). Over the past 45 years, athletes have gotten closer to this goal by only six minutes. The following article describes Sri Chinmoy's view on how to break through this barrier. What is most surprising is that he doesn't put much emphasis on the training techniques or miles per week, but on the inner qualities of the athlete!

The current (2014) world record for the men's marathon is 2 hours 2 minutes and 57 seconds. The 2 hour and 30 minute barrier was broken in 1925. In 1969 Derek Clayton of Australia broke 2 hours and nine minutes. In the past 35 years only 5 minutes and 40 seconds have been taken off that record. Eighteen men have run under 2 hours and 8 minutes!

Marathon 1:59:59
By Sujantra McKeever

It was a Saturday evening in November 1998. An excited hush fell over the crowd of 600 men and women, as spiritual teacher Sri Chinmoy quietly entered a high-school auditorium in Queens, New York. The next day, 370 of his students would be at the starting line for the 26.2-mile New York City Marathon. Many of his students who would not be running would be helping at the aid stations and finish line.

Sri Chinmoy, poet, musician and athlete, was 67 years old, stood 5'7" and weighed 144 pounds. He walked humbly to the front of the room wearing a red and blue track suit, carrying a handful of papers. They were part of a literary marathon he was currently working on which was to span 77,000 poems. Sri Chinmoy took his seat and smiled.

Students of Sri Chinmoy had gathered from more than 25 countries to spend the weekend with their teacher and take part in the New York City marathon. The evening's activities the night before the race included storytelling, music and meditation. Sri Chinmoy meditated with the runners in groups according to how fast they anticipated running the race. He began with the slowest runners. As it turned out, the slowest runner would take eight hours and 30 minutes, while the fastest, a young man from Russia, would complete the race in two hours and 28 minutes.

At last the fastest runners—those trying to break 3 hours, sat down to meditate. Sri Chinmoy looked over the 18 athletes and fell into a deep, meditative silence. A feeling of peaceful, yet powerful energy swept through the room. These runners had spent many months in preparation for the race. Through the power of meditation, their nervousness and anticipation was

being transformed into dynamic enthusiasm and focused excitement. A profound silence and joy coursed through minds and hearts of all present.

Emerging from his meditation, Sri Chinmoy opened his eyes, looked over the runners and began to speak on one of his favourite running topics: the sub two-hour marathon. For the next 20 minutes, he talked about his heart-felt conviction that it would be possible for one of his students, or someone else, to break the two-hour barrier. He said it could be done on 60 miles a week of training if a certain state of awareness and consciousness could be attained. Sri Chinmoy gave utmost importance to the role that spirit and mind play in sports, creative undertakings and daily activities.

In his youth, Sri Chinmoy was a decathlon champion in his native India. Since coming to America in 1964, he worked tirelessly to unite the spiritual ideals of the ancient East with the modern Western world. He conveyed his message through art, prose, poetry, music, meditation and athletics. He performed his meditative music in concerts to millions around the world, always without charge.

Sri Chinmoy loved athletics. He ran 22 marathons and participated in several ultra-marathons. He was also an avid tennis player and weightlifter. He inspired his students to organize running races for their local communities around the world. These races include track and field competitions for senior citizens, two-mile fun runs, marathons, and ultra-marathons ranging from 12 and 24-hour races to a 3,100-Mile multi-day race.

Everyone in the room listened with rapt attention as Sri Chinmoy began to speak on the sub two-hour marathon, an achievement many deem impossible. The intensity was heightened because he said that one of those present could be the one to break the longstanding barrier. Sri Chinmoy elaborated on four achievements necessary to create the state of consciousness to run such a race. The ideas he offered can be applied to any activity in which one wishes to excel.

1. Sri Chinmoy said that during training runs, the athlete must consciously offer gratitude to Mother Earth. Over the years he consistently pointed toward gratitude as an emotion through which individuals can reach their highest potential. "Gratitude," he wrote, "is a miracle-action in us. This miracle-action strengthens our physical body, purifies our vital energy, widens our mental vision and intensifies our psychic delight."

By "Mother Earth" Sri Chinmoy referred not just to the physical planet upon which we live, but also to the deeper Spirit, which creates, sustains and transforms (through birth and death) all of creation. God, according to Sri Chinmoy, has two aspects: masculine and feminine. It is the feminine aspect that brings forth and sustains existence and ourselves.

2. The second idea Sri Chinmoy spoke of is that the runner must aspire toward, attain and sustain peace of mind. Peace is another quality to which he gives utmost importance. Sri Chinmoy often refers to himself as a "student of peace." He said, "No price is too great to pay for inner peace. Peace is the harmonious control of life. It is vibrant with life-energy." The athlete must learn to tap into this life-energy if he or she wishes to transcend past performances. It is only through a calm and serene mind that this energy can be found and then utilized.

The great American sage Ralph Waldo Emerson said, "Nothing can bring you peace but yourself." True peace springs forth when our mind is calm and tranquil. Sri Chinmoy said that lasting satisfaction and calmness stem from true detachment. This is not detachment from daily responsibilities, for these we

must embrace to be good and true citizens of the world. The detachment he speaks of is from the thoughts that steal away our inner peace.

Sri Chinmoy noted, "The greatest misfortune that can come to a human being is to lose his inner peace. No outer force can rob him of it. It is his own thoughts, his own actions that rob him of it."

In order to attain peace in our minds, we must rise above fear, jealousy, insecurity, anger and any other destructive thoughts that threaten the potential stillness of our minds.

An uplifting silence prevailed over the runners as they listened to Sri Chinmoy's words. He was describing a path toward a reality overflowing with potential. The surety of his vision has many times challenged and defeated convention. As Einstein said, "Imagination is more important than knowledge."

3. The third issue Sri Chinmoy addressed is the necessity for the runner to have purity in the vital. In Sri Chinmoy's philosophy, the "vital" describes the emotional and sexual dimension of the human being. Purity is clarity, calmness and a focused intensity toward one's goals. By bringing purity into our vital energy, we can realise and utilise the unlimited source of energy from which we are created and to which we are all connected.

Sri Chinmoy described this purity as "the feeling of a living shrine deep in the inmost recesses of your heart." Purified vital energy becomes manifest as enthusiasm and eagerness, two qualities essential for success in any noble endeavour. As the poet Tennyson wrote, "My strength is as the strength of ten because my heart is pure."

Sri Chinmoy paused and looked out at those gathered for the race. Earlier in the day they had spent four hours putting together the 31,000 bag lunches that are given to the marathon runners as they cross the finish line in Central Park. Many of those present would assist runners after the race and help pick up trash in the park till late the next evening.

4. The fourth and final piece of advice Sri Chinmoy offered is the necessity of bringing discipline into the physical body. Without discipline in the body, one merely rides the pendulum between pleasure and pain. Many people spend their lives doing little else but seeking comfort and pleasure and trying to avoid pain. In order to bring forward our highest potential, we must transcend and transform the body's desires so that our spirit can utilize the body to manifest our unimagined capacities. This is best summed up in a poem Sri Chinmoy wrote.

You can enjoy a limitless life of glory
If you do not allow
Your life to be bound
By your body's rules and regulations.

A "limitless life of glory" dawns when we experience the undying spirit, which is the essence and source of our physical existence. The seeker-athlete can learn to infuse the physical consciousness with the spirit's unimaginable force. It is that force which will uplift the runner to new levels of speed and endurance.

Sri Chinmoy finished speaking and gently closed his eyes. A pin-drop silence enveloped the room. Once more he became absorbed in meditation.

All of the team members, save two or three, completed the race the next day. They had been offered more than encouragement and inspiration the night before. They had been shown the golden keys to unlock their true potential as runners and as

human beings. Gratitude, peace, purity and discipline are those keys. Who will have the courage to unlock the door?

Perhaps you.

TRANSCEND OTHERS - PROBLEMS AND SOLUTIONS

Inner Secrets of Achieving Supreme Heights

IT IS THE NATURE OF OUR MIND and our desires to always strive to surpass others. On the one hand, a desire can be considered as a driving force for advancement. Everything would be fine if this desire were not accompanied by such side effects as jealousy, depression, doubt, bad thoughts, bad plans, foul play, etc. But it is the nature of our mind to believe that by surpassing others, we will find joy in life. And while the inner practice says that this approach only leads to failure, we continue to try to make it work in our lives.

What's wrong?

To develop and improve our standard is essential for our fulfilment in life. I said before that we each have a unique and inimitable mission for which we came to earth. But the unfortunate thing is that we alter this mission through our mundane consciousness, our competition with others and—worst of all—by comparing ourselves with others. When we compare, we

always lose our joy because there is always someone who has achieved more than we have. Someone speaks and writes better than we do. Someone knows more than we do, and so on. These comparisons lead to negative emotions, and needless to say, nothing high, profound, enlightening, fulfilling or joyful can come from negative emotions.

What is the way out?

I would like to offer one profound statement:

"If I want to transcend others, then I must see only their good qualities and make these my very own."[23]

In addition to our training courses, study and other things to educate ourselves, a turn to an inner approach will give us an unimaginable advantage and open wide avenues for development! Just think, if we use the oneness of our spiritual heart, we can claim as our own all the wonderful qualities that others have had from birth or that they have developed over the years.

Another important part of this message, to see other's good qualities, is extremely difficult. But it is not often that we set ourselves such a goal! Try it. You will see how the world around you changes.

And for those readers who would like to use the ability of their spiritual heart to develop their identification with others, oneness and a positive approach to life, I recommend a selection of meditation exercises, visualisations and many of the inspirational videos at *www.SriChinmoy.tv*

OTHER BOOKS BY STUTISHEEL

Eat to Run. Holistic nutrition for the ultra marathon runner. CreateSpace Independent Publishing Platform; 3rd edition, 2014

My First Ironman. From dream to finish. CreateSpace Independent Publishing Platform, 2015

Run. Journey. Become. The 3100-mile footrace of a lifetime. CreateSpace Independent Publishing Platform; first edition, 2016

Books are available in paperback and kindle format at www.Amazon.com

FOOTNOTES

1. *A Guide to the Project Management Body of Knowledge*. Project Management Institute.

2. Sri Chinmoy, *My Meditation-Service at the United Nations for 25 Years*. Agni Press, 1995.

3. Sri Chinmoy, *Mind-Confusion and Heart-Illumination, Part 2*. Agni Press, 1974.

4. Sri Chinmoy, *Silence Calls Me*. Agni Press, New York, 1993

5. Sri Chinmoy, *Seventy-Seven Thousand Service-Trees, Part 15*. Agni Press, 1999.

6. Kotter, John, *Power and Influence*. Free Press, New York, 2008.

7. Sri Chinmoy, *A Sri Chinmoy Primer*. Agni Press, 1974.

8. Rogers, Carl R., *Toward a Theory of Creativity*. Boston, Houghton Mifflin, 1989.

9. Sri Chinmoy, *The Body: Humanity's Fortress*. Agni Press, 1974.

10. Sri Chinmoy, *Meditations: Food for the Soul*. Agni Press, 1970

11. Sri Chinmoy, *Peace-Blossom-Fragrance, Part 3*. Agni Press, 1994.

12. Sri Chinmoy, *My Christmas-New Year-Vacation Aspiration-Prayers, Part 51*. Agni Press, 2007.

13. Sri Chinmoy, *Sri Chinmoy Answers, Part 32*. Agni Press,

New York, 2002.

14. Sri Chinmoy, *Meditation: God Speaks and I Listen, Part 2*. Agni Press, 1974.

15 Sri Chinmoy, *The Wings of Joy: Finding Your Path to Inner Peace*. Simon & Schuster, New York, 1997.

16. Sri Aurobindo, *Letters On Yoga, Volume 3, Part 4*. Lotus Press, Pondicherry, 1988.

17. Sri Chinmoy, *Ten Thousand Flower-Flames, Part 38*. Agni Press, New York, 1982.

18. Sri Chinmoy, *Aum Magazine, Oct. 1976, p. 1-3*. Sri Chinmoy Centre, New York.

19. Sri Chinmoy, *Meditate On, Jharna-Kala Card Co.*, New York, 1995.

20. Sri Chinmoy, *The Oneness of the Eastern Heart and the Western Mind, Part 2*. Agni Press, New York, 2004.

21. Sri Chinmoy, *The Source of Music*. Aum Publications, New York, 1995.

22. Sri Chinmoy, *Sri Chinmoy Speaks, Part 4*. Agni Press, 1976.

23. Sri Chinmoy, *The Oneness of the Eastern Heart and the Western Mind, Part 3*. Agni Press, New York, 2004.